OVER

the

RAINBOW

{Your Guide to living the life of your dreams}

~ i ~

Debbie Dixon

Tony—
I am so glad to see
all of your dreams
coming true. You continue
to amaze me.

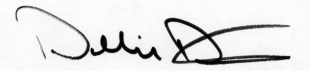

ISBN: 1491250690
ISBN-13: 9781491250693

I dedicate this book to all those beings that live their life in service. Those who give each day to the purpose of bringing more joy into the lives of others!

Lokah Samasta Sukhino Bhavantu
May all beings everywhere be happy and free and may the thoughts, words and actions of my own life contribute in some way to that happiness and to that freedom for all.

Over the Rainbow

CONTENTS

Over the Rainbow

Over the Rainbow

ACKNOWLEDGMENTS

This book is a compilation of love and devotion. Although I had spent my whole life researching and preparing, I couldn't have completed the book without the assistance from many angels along the way. Through divine guidance and endless hours, I poured onto these pages a recipe for living your life on purpose, with passion. So many have come to the aid of this creation and I find myself in the deepest gratitude for each and every one of them. Each individual held a very special part in creating the whole. Chris and Mike Manning, Jason Coleman, Jason Maples, Chad Bickle, Kurt Rahrig, Michael Uslan, Yusuf Saad, have all inspired me at one point or another to keep going. My children Keegan and Dallas gave the gift of time to the book. They understood when I would disappear to my room for hours and for the most part let me be. I would also like to say thank you to Lori Snyder for her assistance with the editing. Lastly, I wish to thank all of you that have read my book and helped me to refine my message. Most of all I wish to thank all of my many wonderful teachers and guides who have assisted me on my path!

Prologue

I have discovered a map that will guide you from wherever you are, to where ever you want to be! When I found this map and saw the life of my dreams had been hidden right under my nose, I realized that a treasure is without value unless I can share it with others. I am no different than anybody else. Yet, I have unraveled the mystery and on these pages, unveiled the path to living the life of your dreams, free from fear, anger, guilt and frustration. A life that is free to become in an instant, whatever your heart desires.

I grew up in the typical, all-American, upper middle class family: three kids and a dog. The only thing missing was the white picket fence. But, within my house dwelled pain, fear, sadness, and struggle. As a child who was both sexually and emotionally abused, the answers for me were not simple nor a fairy tale. I found myself trapped in the cycle of escaping one hell, just to find myself in another. I became a mother at age seventeen. Homeless and desperate, I found comfort in abusive relationships. It was what I knew. The harder I tried to dig my way out, the deeper the hole seemed to get.

Eventually I hit the bottom. I, like so many, had an internal guidance system that had been damaged when I was very young. The human DNA is written to search for love and happiness. This is necessary for survival and intrinsic to human nature. Like the monarch butterfly is born with its destination written into its DNA. Its survival depends on its migration over 2,500 miles every year. Without a guide or a map, it just knows the way.

I had been broken before I was strong enough to fly.

Imagine the butterfly with a wing that never fully develops. The world had caused my guidance system to malfunction. While most were flying towards love and happiness I had landed in fear and isolation mistaking it for love. I joined many others with broken wings in the heart of the underworlds; where sex, prostitution, abuse, and drugs permeated the air. Although all of the people trapped in the confines of rock bottom shared the same desire for love sketched into their DNA, they had never been shown what it looks like. It became the blind leading the blind, in the dark.

Rock bottom is a place where life exists in the shadows. Lost souls, with broken wings unable to fly, wander looking for love in fame and fortune, pain is accepted as a way of life.

I witnessed rock bottom and it looked much like what the media is glorifying as the destination we are trying to arrive at. I was there in the midst of celebrities. I attended parties in penthouses and mansions. I worked all over the United States; Hawaii, Alaska, Florida, Nevada, California, Oregon, Arizona, Montana and Washington. I was featured in movies, television, magazines and commercials I was even in the National Enquirer alongside Halle Berry. To most, my life may have looked glamorous. In reality, I was surrounded by sleaze, debauchery, hollow, lost and soulless people who emanated hurt and pain. I watched many walk this very fine line.

On one side you give up your soul, which your body needs for survival, the other side is a journey of blind faith, made on foot until you can mend your wing. Often those walking the line would slip and fall, never to be seen again. Swallowed up by the monster labeled "fame and fortune," resulting in the sacrificing of their soul and the separation from their selfless, true nature towards a life of need, greed and speed.

Fear lead to struggle, which lead me right off the edge. Once at the bottom, I had seen with my own eyes the monster that had eaten many of my friends. I think that was exactly what I had needed all along, to look the monster directly in its eyes and say "I am not scared of you! I know life is good and I intend to prove it to the world!" As I pulled myself out of the darkness and climbed up the mountain of joy, I often looked back and wondered, "why was I able to do it while I am leaving behind so many still lost and lonely?" My curiosity continued to grow leaving me in a constant state of wonder about humans and our capability.

This wonder has led me to the feet of many masters and hundreds of books, searching for answers. Over the last 16 years, I have immersed myself in self-inquiry through the practices of yoga and meditation. About 7 years ago I made the transition from student to teacher. As a teacher I had seen people embarking on the climb up the same mountain I had once scaled, and I was able to assist them on their path.

I have been to the place that most never return whole from and I have brought back a message I must share. These pages hold that message. I woke up one day, looked around, and found myself nestled among those our society looks upon with disapproval. I realized I was no different. I intend to show you a story of triumph over the confines of jail and drugs, pain and fear.

I have transcended from this dark world and discovered a magical formula that allows me to stand in the very same shoes, in the very same location and see a whole different world. This new world is one of beauty and love, compassion and kindness everywhere I look. I have written this book with the prayer that you will witness my journey and watch your world change right in front of your eyes!

Section One

It is the dream that gives us the journey…but, the journey that gives us the joy!

my story

Over the Rainbow

CHAPTER ONE

~Dreams Can Be Your Reality~

Have you ever dreamed something so outrageous, just for the sake of self-trickery, and for a split second an almost unfathomable life story seemed true? Did you notice when you tried to remember it, the details of the dream become lost in the land of impossibility?

What if dreaming the impossible dream enough times begins to make the impossible possible? This book will reestablish the art of dreaming into your everyday regimen. You will once again see the world as a place of infinite possibilities. Upon completion of this book, you will be armed with tools to change the way you think, feel, see, and experience your world. Get prepared to have your entire life experience change. Veils will be lifted, and a whole new world will be revealed, this is the world as you were truly intended to see it.

To open up to new concepts, ideas, and thought processes, a commitment to being a good student is necessary. In order to absorb new information, the heart and the mind must be open. There is a Buddhist parable that begins with a disciple asking his master how to find Zen. Instead of answering, the master hands the disciple an empty glass, picks up a pitcher filled with water, and begins to pour the water in the glass. The master continues pouring until the glass overflows with water, and yet he still pours on. The disciple, very disturbed, exclaims, "Master, the glass is full! Why do you keep pouring water?" The master puts down the pitcher and responds, "My son, this is what you are asking me to do: place more into a mind that is already full. You must first empty your mind. Then you will find Zen."

Before embarking on the grand new venture this book is presenting, try to empty your mind and create a beautiful pasture, rich with nourishing soil for the seeds of new intentions and affirmative ways of thinking. Let the mind be an open and expansive space where light can easily sprout ripe and bountiful fruits. With a willingness to learn and an open mind to receive new concepts and ideas, this book can and will change your life.

To maximize the benefits you will receive from absorbing the contents of this book, take time to truly ponder these next few questions. Write your answers in a notebook and keep this notebook by your side to use for the worksheets throughout the book.

Ask Yourself…

~Do you intend to have abundance, happiness and joy?
~Are you ready to prosper in all areas of your life?
~Are you ready to have what you want?
~Are you ready to learn to magnetize money to you?

As you read on, keep in mind the answers you wrote down…and watch your world miraculously change as you rediscover the power that you had all along.

CHAPTER TWO

~Life: A Series of Intentions~

Every journey begins with the first step. Imagine, within your brain is uncharted territory, brand new terrain. This hidden part of the brain can only operate from the standpoint of a clear understanding that you are the creator of your circumstances. Stake claim of this new territory and know the view from this expansive new land will change every aspect of your current understanding of the way life works. Having taken the first step, staked claim of this new world, you must stand in the midst of your creation, look around you and own the possibility that everything you see, began in your mind as a thought. If you can accept and believe that, then it suffices to say that if you wanted to see something else, you would have to start by thinking something else. What do you wish to see? Ask yourself and then intend it to be.

Setting intentions for the outcome of any situation, long term or short term, is how you take ownership of your life. Setting intentions says that you have control over your own destiny. That you create your reality and this is how it will look. You can shift from a mere passenger in your life to being the driver. Most of us have the belief that life happens to us…and, to an extent, this is true. When you set an intention, it focuses only on the outcome; it does not fill in the pieces of how you will arrive there. The beauty is that you don't have to know the how.

Intentions are the secret of the masters, people who have conquered what seem to be impossible feats. If you intend to have something and stay true to that intention, it will be! You will just have to carefully guard your thoughts, consistently keeping them in line with your intention. For example, you cannot intend to have a million dollars all the while, consistently thinking "I will never have a million dollars; I have nothing but bills everywhere!" You have to set the intention with blind faith that it will be.

Let me fill you in on a little secret: rarely will you be able to see any link at all between your dream and your reality! You will have to rely solely on imagination and creativity as you launch your intention with absolutely no evidence that it is conceivable. This is why so few stay on track and realize their dreams.

The people that set world records didn't know the how. They couldn't know the how as it had never been done before! They just knew their intent, and they set their expectations to exceed what their eyes and ears, told them was possible. In this moment, the intent was created: seeing the result you want is all it takes. See it, feel it, and release it to the universe. The universe will leap into action, laying each step in front of you to create the perfect circumstances for you to achieve your intention.

The gold metal doesn't just arrive. You must follow the steps as they are shown to you. The steps may look like a lot of work, but to the person who sees the end result as if it has already arrived, the steps feel like living for the first time! You will be filled with passion and enthusiasm. When walking the path towards a divinely inspired intention, joy fills the body and people and things are drawn to you like a magnet. You start to feel energized and full of "joie de vivre", zest for life. This is why we all need to know what our intent is with this day! What do you intend to create today?

You already live within the creation of your intentions.

Up until now this has been an involuntary action of your subconscious. You intend on waking up and having breakfast. You intend to arrive at work. Little intentions are being set all day in your mind without your conscious awareness. Take charge! Become more conscious of your intentions. Don't just intend to arrive at work; intend to have a peaceful drive there and arrive refreshed and full of energy! Intend to have a fun, productive day with supportive coworkers.

By setting your intention, you are consciously stating what you want to experience in every situation. You are aligning your mind with the universal law of attraction that says whatever you request under this law has to be granted to you! By making this a regular practice you can create, with clarity, the life of your choice.

I know what it is like living with the belief that life is happening to you, what it is like to pray that the single thread holding it all together will stay strong enough to buy just one more day, what it is like living with thoughts filled with worries of "what if?" I had allowed life to happen to me for many years. I lived believing that life was a series of unfortunate, uncontrollable events, and any choice I had only consisted of the better of two evils. The life I knew was unreliable and would consistently let me down, and my expectations remained in that swirling vortex of unhappiness. Setting an intention or a goal was scary because it opened me up to the possibility of more disappointment, more things that could go wrong. I was better off sticking with the misery that I knew.

If you have experienced similar thoughts, treat them as a signal that you have forgotten you have control over everything within you at all times. With the ingredients in this book you will mix together a formula of intention which will turn your life into the life of your dreams. You will never again live in fear of the thread breaking and everything crumbling around you. This book will build a strong foundation, allowing only good to come to you. Limitless possibilities await you! The winning lottery ticket is always right there in your back pocket and all you have ever needed to do is cash it in. What is holding you back from the flood gates of prosperity finally bursting through those barriers of limitation you continue to reinforce?

The world wants you to believe that you can't have it all. That is what you have been told, because that is what those who guided you were told. Nobody was trying to mislead you on purpose; they thought they were protecting you.

Our world has been overcome with a fast spreading virus affecting our operating systems and forcing us into a sleep from which we never wake. This disease attacks the mind, the body, and the spirit, creating an imagined separation between these areas of ourselves. The virus gains momentum and strength through fear, using mass media. Television and the newspapers are riddled with fear-driven tales of the war, failure, and demise that must come to all who step outside the box. These subtle messages to society tell you that you will not succeed, that there are too many risks, so why bother getting your hopes up when failure is the most likely result? Those behind our media have been infected by the virus, and until they become awakened they will keep spreading it to every person their stories reach.

"Do you think I am trying to weave a spell? Perhaps I am; but remember your fairy tales. Spells are used for breaking enchantments as well as for inducing them. And you and I have need of the strongest spell that can be found to wake us from the evil enchantment of worldliness which has been laid upon us for

nearly a hundred years." C.S. Lewis

The great ones, the ones who live the life of their dreams, are the ones who tune all of that out and decide, with a certain amount of passion and commitment, that no matter what, "It will be." They understand that failure is an illusion and fear cannot exist in this moment. They strive to live in the present moment where fear and lack cannot exist. They stop the virus from reaching them by turning off their television sets and avoiding the top news stories of the day (designed to feed fear), and they go inward to reconnect with their own intuition and guidance.

There is a cure for this virus, and you are well on your way. You are one of the great ones and this is your time to shine. You are at the leading edge of consciousness, on the brink of discovering the cure and bringing it to the masses, for the cure is in these pages. You won't need to travel to a distant land or find some healer to give you the cure because it exists within all of us, all of the time. This book will awaken you and, in recognizing all of the ways this virus has and is affecting your life, you will be able to counter it. Day by day, the virus will grow weaker and your power and inner strength will grow stronger. Make it your intent to rid yourself of fear and unhappiness. Wake up to your truth and finally experience the joy you are here to experience. It is your right!

Remember, these techniques take practice. You have spent years perfecting other ways of thinking and being, so changes might not happen overnight... although intentions possess magic and miracles!

Let's practice writing down a few intentions. You can set an intent for any life experience, small or large. Perhaps start with an upcoming meeting or event, or an intention for the next hour, or day, or for your job or your dream vacation. No intention is too small or too grand!

~How to set an intention~

Examples:

• *My intention for this book is to learn practical ways of transforming my life with ease.*
• *My intention is to have a day filled with effortless and abundant creativity.*
• *My intention for my day is to be peaceful and centered.*
• *My intention for the holiday season is enjoy deep and loving connections of joy and laughter.*

Now, take out your notebook and set your intention for this book.

CHAPTER THREE

~My Beginning:
How Our Paths are Chosen~

"Please. Don't go…"

I knew they couldn't, or wouldn't, hear me. Sometimes as I sat in my invisible bubble, I would contemplate if they were too busy or if I was just that insignificant. I learned very early that making it through the battlefield that was my life, meant I couldn't rely on anyone but myself. That and my books; I had earlier filled a backpack with the books that fueled my imagination and allowed me to transcend the real world. Television was a highly restricted luxury in my childhood home, so thankfully I was forced to rely solely on books for entertainment. I began to love words and their mystifying ability to bring beauty to something otherwise unpleasant.

My mother spent most of her life fixated on the mirror and unaware of my presence. Really, anything with a reflective surface would do. She spent hours every day trying to reach her idea of perfection, making sure every detail had been tended to. Once every hair was in its place and her entire face had been painted, she would take a magnifying glass and get a closer look. At the makeup counter where she worked, she was indistinguishable from all the other over-done, try-not-to-smile-because-it-causes-wrinkles salespeople.

I drove my mother absolutely crazy with my complete disarray. Her admonishments about what a lady should look and act like sounded like a foreign language: "Please don't crinkle your forehead up like that, Debbie. You will get wrinkles. Don't squint your eyes! You'll end up looking just like Linda at the make-up counter. I swear she could lose something in those deep crevices." Even smiling could permanently disfigure me if you were to ask my mom.

To me, combing my hair seemed more like a corporal punishment than daily hygiene. I had two older brothers; bruises and scratches from rough housing were a given. I loved to climb trees and adventure in the woods, which further segregated me from the typical dress-wearing population in my neighborhood.

I would rarely make it straight home from school without an extra adventurous excursion. We lived on a golf course nestled amongst endless canyons; my favorite detour was a spot where rainwater would settle into a creek at the bottom of one of these canyons. It was an ideal place for a hopeless dreamer to create secret societies of tree houses, where magic and miracles were plenty and possibilities ended only with your imagination. I would hop through the creek from stone to stone, hoping this day would be the day I would finally make it to the end without getting wet.

On this particular night, as I begged my mother not to leave, she put on one last coat of lipstick, powdered her face, and gave herself a final once-over before grabbing her purse and making her way to the front door.

Earlier that day, I had overheard my mom on the phone telling a friend that she and my father would be having dinner at the country club. It was enough to send my heart a rush of pure adrenaline and create an anxiety attack, causing the self-preservation mode to take over. Busyness could always take my mind off the fearful thoughts compounding on top of each other that fed my anxiety.

I heard the door knob turn as my parents left, then the humming of the engine as they started the car. As the engine drifted into the distance I knew they were gone and I had to act quickly: I didn't know where he was and wasn't going to let him to catch me. With little time to weigh the options, I decided that the office upstairs, with the lock on the door, might be the best place for tonight. By the time I got there, the panic was in full force. My face was flushed and I could feel the sweat accumulating on my forehead and back. I almost slammed the door shut behind me in the hastiness of my rush, but I caught myself and closed it quietly, taking a deep breath of relief the second I turned the latch on the door. My home was a fortress, with locks present on all the doors, special screws on the molding surrounding the doors, and backup devices such as a wooden stick that fit snuggly between the door handle and the floor.

One of my brothers was a drug addict who shared the typical, lovable qualities of your run-of-the-mill addict: with priorities placed on getting high, there was little time for keeping up with a job. Without money, stealing became necessary to satisfy his habits. Since no one else in the neighborhood allowed my brother anywhere near their home, our parents were his easiest target. While the rest of the neighborhood held secret meetings to discuss how to protect themselves and their children's piggy banks from my brother, my parents installed locks, high-tech alarm systems and not so high tech sticks for windows and doors throughout our entire home.

All of these things were born of and fed fear. In response to my brother's troubles, my home became a place where I never felt completely safe. I didn't grow up with an understanding that home is your warm, soft place to fall when times get tough. My home was the place you wanted to get away from as often as you could.

These were the circumstances that created a cold and dark place in my soul, ideal for the virus of society to take hold. Although it lay dormant, residing in my subconscious, it dictated how I saw the world from that point on. I had succumbed to the ideas of this imagined fear, the idea that the world is filled with people who want to hurt you and take advantage of you. The virus didn't just attack my immune system; it attacked my operating system as well. I spent many years suffering from this ailment of the mind, body, and spirit.

"To dream by night is to escape your life. To dream by day is to make it happen." Stephen Richards

The night my parents left, Tony, the druggie, was in juvenile hall. I was alone with him. Locked in the office, I kicked up the security systems a notch, adding the super deluxe defense stick under the door knob to prevent anyone from being able to push the door open. Then I found sanctuary in the closet, along with my backpack of books. The only light came from under the door, which made reading challenging, but the feeling of vulnerability had been greatly reduced.

"Where are you?"

In that instance, all the imagined safety I had conjured came crashing down around me. It was as if the walls had crumbled and I was left exposed, completely unprotected in enemy territory. It wouldn't take him long to find me, and if I didn't cooperate and just open the door, I knew he would punish me. Also, I knew he was upset. Even at this very young age, I could sense people's energy, and as a child who felt better inside when everyone around her was happy, I would find myself doing things that resulted in a temporary moment of relief from everyone else's discomfort, even if it hurt me.

It is an interesting phenomenon how quickly things can change. In the blink of an eye, the room that had been my sanctuary seemed to take the smallest sound and magnify it to the hundredth degree. It was as if the room itself was screaming here she is, come get her! My breathing, just moments before completely unnoticeable, now sounded louder than a jet airplane. Holding my breath was worse, because when I did finally gasp for air I was terrified he could hear.

"Are you in there? What are you doing? Open the door. Stop being silly, I have a surprise for you."

HA! I wasn't going to fall for that one again, although I knew he was telling the truth and I was a little curious about the surprise. He always lured me with some sort of bait and knew that, with a wild imagination and gentle simplicity, I would settle for playing with the bubbles in the sink. Having access to this insider's knowledge, he would frequently use this as one of his prizes, letting me use the dish soap and fill the whole sink with bubbles….as long as I did what he wanted first. Sometimes he would even have money, or let me watch what I wanted to on the television.

I had my coping techniques as well, mainly consisting of getting it over with so it could be hidden in the past. Sometimes he would set the egg timer, and when it beeped I could be done and claim my prize. I liked that the best because it gave me something to focus on and I could see it counting down feeling relief as each second passed.

That sense of security perished the day the egg timer sounded its virtuous alarm of salvation and he didn't stop. When it was all over, the ritualistic discussion surrounding the topic of secrecy would take place. First thing on the agenda; I was under strict instructions to never tell my mom and dad. He informed me that they would be very angry, and punish me severely. I could never comprehend what made him think I would ever want to tell. I had a tremendous amount of guilt and shame and I lived in a smile, disguising guilt and shame. The haunting fear of the disappointment and disgust my parents would shower on me if they knew, assured this would stay my secret forever.

This was the way the world was shown to me as a child. I didn't know anything else. I thought everyone had a life filled with similar experiences and circumstances. It wasn't until I realized that the world didn't have to look the way I was shown it, that I was on the path towards truth.

CHAPTER FOUR

~How I Changed the Past and Recreated my Future~

Each of our paths hold a vastly different story with a unique story teller; Choices born of society's virus affects each of our lives to varying degrees, depending on who is telling the story and where this story is taking place. The climax of all of our stories create the same outcome, a bump in the road or a gentle nudge from a stranger causes you to stop dead in your tracks, with nowhere else to go, your journey turns inward. From that new perspective the storyteller is the same in all of us; we discover that we all share the same pain, fear, and heartbreak with the same desire to feel a connection to something. Our paths may look different from the outside; but, they all lead to the same destination (our hearts). This is your nudge. Go inward and discover that the antidote to society's virus starts by drinking a spoonful of acceptance, non-judgment, oneness, understanding and chasing it with unconditional love.

Remind yourself; If it looks like judgment and talks like judgment, it probably is judgment. Stop judging!

Life is viewed as something we experience outwardly. We look outside ourselves for the cause of our pain and discomfort, blaming everyone else. It isn't until we start to look inward that we take on a new understanding, seeing that everything external is just a manifestation of where it all began: our thoughts.

For all of us, inherently, our deepest desire is to have pure, unconditional love, and a sense of oneness or belonging. On the quest for meaning, we undoubtedly experience small doses of the cure and quick glimpses of awakening. An unsolicited smile from a stranger or finding yourself on the receiving end of an unexpected act of kindness is a glimmer of light in the dark. These moments hold opportunities for healing through the experience of love and acceptance. Joy, compassion, and understanding—even in small doses—can subdue the virus, allowing the path to become clear.

The path I refer to is a journey of revelations that will purify your soul and cleanse your body and mind. This is the path on which we release all attachments; we strip ourselves of judgments and labels. When we do this, it becomes clear that under all of the stuff, emotional baggage, and material possessions that we have accumulated over the years, we are exactly the same. We have the same basic wants and needs, and we are all cut from the exact same love.

It is when we connect with our highest selves that we can honor the place within each of us where the universe dwells, the place that is of love, of light, of peace and of truth. When you are in that place within, and I am in that place within, we are one. Namaste.

Life is a journey to enlightenment. The goal is ascension and freedom from suffering. Desires are little nuggets that we use as motivation, to guide us towards a deeper understanding of what is really important, the proverbial carrot. Needs are the imaginary fears that hold us back and keep us stagnant. The key to happiness lies in the present moment.

To realize that in this moment all of your needs are met and you are whole is to have discovered the key to life. You will have awakened and cured the virus affecting society. Each time you find a desire and release a need, you will move up the ladder of ascension into a deeper sense of awakening. Sometimes, before we begin to rise, it may seem as though we have fallen even further. This was true for me.

"In their innocence, very young children know themselves to be light and love. If we will allow them, they can teach us to see ourselves the same way." Michael Jackson

A dear friend of mine once said to me, "It can be tempting to jump over the canyon and pretend it doesn't exist, but the cure is buried there. To find it, you must employ an expedition and navigate through the rocky terrain, waterfalls and raging rivers. The cure resides somewhere in a dark cave, and you must dive into the depths of the ravine to find it."

This was certainly true for me. As I began my search, I found myself questioning everything I had, until that point, accepted as reality. What felt like several lifetimes of experiences and knowledge had to be analyzed and reconsidered. Thoughts of "Why am I here? What is the meaning of life?" were beginning to weigh on me. To find the answers, I knew I needed to return to the place it all began, so I took a trip to the beginning, the house where I had grown up.

All grown, I sat outside my childhood home, in the midst of my old neighborhood, the place that had both housed the infinite possibilities of life and, in the same breath, taken them away. I was there for the sake of reconnecting with the infinite possibilities we hold as children. I wanted to remember what that felt like. At first, the neighborhood didn't seem familiar. It felt strange, everything different: new paint, some new shrubs in the front. Before, it had been an earthy light tan with subtle yellow hues. Now it seemed brazen with its new bright barn-red color. The new owners had added one of those mailboxes that looks a miniature version of the house, and hung a sign over the door that said "The Pittsons." I wondered what kind of family the Pittsons were.

I decided it might be easier to look for the similarities, the things that haven't changed. At a glance the neighborhood seemed untouched by time. Yet something about it was distinctly different. Why did it feel so different? I had to draw the conclusion that the lenses I was looking through were the difference. It was me who had changed, not my old neighborhood.

As I looked at it now, everything seemed smaller and more insignificant. The giant mansion I had grown up in looked like a regular house, maybe even a little on the insignificant side. I became conscious in that moment to the truth that our perceptions create what we see. That truth revealed Answer Number One to those very powerful questions I had raised.

What we see and how we define our experiences, is unilateral and biased.

There are at least two different versions to every situation, two different ways to hear and see every story. In fact, there are as many perceptions or different experiences as there are people having the experience. No two perceptions of a person, place or thing will ever be exactly the same. Someone else could have easily seen my old house and thought "What a wonderful place to raise a family." It was my past that changed the way I was viewing the present.

As soon as I realized this, I tried observing everything as though I was seeing it for the very first time, with absolutely no judgment. To my amazement, a new world transformed right before my eyes, into a miraculous place filled with endless escapades of joy-filled experiences. If I didn't use my past to place fear into my anticipation of the future, I found freedom and a limitless view on my possible future, encapsulated with a sense of excitement and wonder.

What is clouding your perception? When you look at the world, do you have an expectation about it, created by stories you have lived, read, been told or imagined? Can you imagine how the world around you might look different if you could see it free from the preconceived notions or opinions established through life's trials and tribulations? The truth is, most of the judgments you have acquired throughout your life aren't even established by you. Rather, you have likely formed opinions based on what other people conveyed to you as being important for your survival. As a child, experiences may have been forced upon you without your choice or permission, creating beliefs about life. Most of your opinions, perceptions and ideas are formed and given to you by those who held a position of influence in your formative years.

If you were visiting this planet for the first time or seeing it through the eyes of a newborn, would your beliefs still hold value? Do those beliefs, without the stories that established them, matter at all? Sometimes it can be difficult to allow ourselves to see things differently from everyone else, but this is the porthole to expansion, discovery, inventions and revelations! Don't forget, there was a time when the earth was thought to be flat. It took just a couple courageous individuals to disbelieve what they were told and set out to prove otherwise, and they were ridiculed and sometimes even killed. But now the world is viewed differently because these courageous few chose to not accept others' truth as their own.

What is a belief?

A belief is nothing more than a thought that you have had so many times that now it has become an expectation or truth. Once we have found a belief, our life experience begins to mimic back to us verification and hard evidence that this belief is true. Just as you look into the mirror and see yourself exactly as you are, your life is a giant mirror reflecting back to you every thought, feeling, emotion you are having. Your mirror does not have the ability to choose sides. In fact, your experience itself cannot recognize the difference between a good and bad experience, because good and bad are perceptions based on the perceiver's programming. The belief "all men cheat" or "nobody will ever love me" would assign your life the plot of victim or adulterer. Have you noticed how the woman who has an abusive husband or boyfriend will free herself of that relationship only to find another man that will treat her the same way? She has to change her belief before she can change the story of her life.

You change your reality and your experience by recognizing the belief that you have, following it to its origin, the place where it was first conceived, and then changing it. If you believe "You are lovable and loved," or "Monogamy is an important aspect of a relationship," you will intrinsically be drawn to the people and things who give evidence that those beliefs are true. In other words, it really doesn't matter what belief you choose. They will all be true. So choose wisely.

At fifteen, I would create a belief that I couldn't count on anyone but myself. This became the prescription for the lenses through which I saw the world. Everywhere I looked, the world reflected this belief back to me. Knowing I could count only on myself, I found ways to release from my life everyone close to me who tried to lend me a hand in times of need, to verify that I couldn't count on them.

The world seemed to continue creating an undeniable wall of evidence proving me right. I was trying to convince myself that I was worthy, blocking myself from receiving unconditional support. This was a constant source of unfulfilling dissatisfaction in my life. I had decided that I couldn't count on my parents to help me, so I was pushed from my home. I decided that I couldn't count on my son's dad, so I created a situation that proved that to be true. With a "me against the world" attitude, I easily found myself doing whatever it took to get by.

Life bore a strong resemblance to a battle field. So, I packed on the armor. Over the years the battles grew bigger and I came more prepared. To feel safe and protected meant more layers of armor; eventually its weight became unbearable. Creation relies on assistance. You can only do so much on your own. It takes an army to create an empire. The belief I can do it all on my own took big dreams and shrunk them to the size of one person. It takes 100's of people just to get the orange on the shelf at the store. The help of others is crucial in living the life of your dreams.

What came first, the chicken or the egg?

Most of us believe that we have our beliefs because of the evidence. But, when we take the time to track the belief back to its origin, it is clear that the belief has been nourishing itself to stay alive ever since the moment it was first conceived. If you want your life to change, you must start by recognizing your beliefs and where they originated.

pull your beliefs out by the roots and plant something new in the fertile soil.

When you revisit that place or time in your life when the seed was planted, look for the differences. Take the belief you established and ask yourself if the opposite might be true. For example, is it possible that, although you were told that you were stupid as a child and all of your memories reaffirm you were stupid. Can you prove the opposite statement true as well and find evidence in your life to prove it? Can you actively search for and see the moments where your intelligence shined? Can you see the amazing contributions that child is here to offer the world?
If you were to change your belief to say "I was perfect and whole exactly as I was," could you search your memory banks and prove that statement to be true? Were there times where you were told you were smart? Now, as you move through life with this new belief, how do you feel? Begin to rewrite your history telling a whole new story. Find a new perspective that serves who you want to become.

When you are on the path to Realizing your Dreams, the universe is going to test you, building the strength of a true warrior to make sure that you are strong enough to move through the turbulent energies as you transcend

When I revisit my childhood in my mind now, I see that my parents were there for me the best way they knew how to be. They didn't want to support the lifestyle I was choosing and they were not properly armed with the ammunition or advise to direct me down a new path. They didn't understand why I had chosen the path I did. They could see me only through the prescription that life had placed on their lenses.

There are as many sides to every story as there are people having the experience.

The study of debate is positioned around the concept of, developing the ability to play from either side of a topic with equal ease. There isn't a topic that cannot be debated. Recognizing this as true, you must ask yourself which side of the debate you choose. I urge you to choose your side based on which one makes you feel happier and more at ease. This is true with everything in life! Pick any belief you would like to have now and start to look for evidence that it is true. Pretend that you are in a debate and you are proving your side. All of these stories are out there. We are just not seeing them because we are still proving our other beliefs to be true.

The ease of money to flow in and out of your life represents the ease of life energy to flow through you.

Ask yourself what beliefs you have around money. Money is our national currency. It is energy, bringing with it the power to create. Start to notice if you have surrounded yourself with people that verify your beliefs, mirroring them back to you. Do your friends complain about never having enough money? Do you notice people at the store complaining about how much things cost? Are you finding yourself surrounded by thoughts of "There isn't enough to go around?"

Are these beliefs working for you? If these beliefs are not working for you and you wish to change them, choose to change them! Believe that you have financial freedom and that money flows to you easily and effortlessly. Create the belief that you can have love and money, and that money flows into your life with a loving energy, and you can lovingly return it into the circulation of the planet. Once you have started to pay attention to your beliefs, you are really ready to start practicing The Law of Attraction.

One of my earliest and most prominent beliefs about money was "money flows to me through means of my sexuality." I was in a Seminar for Nuero Linguistic Programming and I was asked to write down my very first experience with money and was mortified as this belief poured out of my pen onto the paper. This belief began a long struggle between me wanting to prove to the world that I had more value than my sexuality, while drawing money to myself through my sexuality.

Money had also played a large role in my innocence being stolen as a child. Money was used as a bargaining tool by my abuser to keep me from telling. Or he would hide money on his body and ask me to search for it and say that I could keep it. Not that there was every really a choice; it wasn't It wasn't as though I could say "no, thanks" to the money and then not suffer the abuse. I had established several beliefs about myself and the world through these experiences. One of the other prominent and long lasting beliefs was the belief that money was dirty and had negativity attached to it. I never spent the money that he gave me; in fact, I hid it in my room and prayed no one would ever find it. I lived in fear that I would have to explain where it had come from. In my early adult years I continued this tradition. For years I would find money that I had hidden in a shoe, shirt pocket, under the mattress, or even randomly placed in books, squashed between the pages.

In a society where money is our currency, our beliefs about money create our belief about our worth and significance in the world. It is crucial that you know your beliefs on an intimate level.

What you love you empower
and what you fear you empower -
and what you empower you attract.
~ Author Unknown ~

The day I exposed the belief, that my worth was my sexuality, was the day I found true freedom. That was the clog in my drain. I was finally liberated from proving, living, and verifying a belief that, for my whole life, had been holding me back from being who I truly was, my authentic self. From that moment forward, everything changed.

If you wonder why everything that you want is somewhere just out of your reach, there is always a belief at the core of your stagnancy. When you feel as though you are standing in quicksand, each step getting harder and harder to take until you finally give up because your legs can't make the journey, look at what beliefs you are holding onto that tell you, you can't fly. The moment of revelation brings a shift in your body, and all that is left to do is take action. You will feel the lightness in your step once again.

When I discovered my belief about money and scanned my life from the moment of the inception of that belief to the present day, the pattern was obvious. The easiest way to find a belief you have established is look for the patterns. In my adult years my sexuality became my sole means to make money.

"You are given the gifts of the gods: you create your reality according to your beliefs. Yours is the creative energy that makes your world. There are no limitations to the self except those you believe in." Seth (as channeled by Jane Roberts) in 'The Nature Of Personal Reality"

CHAPTER FIVE

~The Karma Bank~

Jail is a good sign that you have encountered a steady decline and it's time to start making some strides back up the mountain. In my young adult years, I made several choices that went against my good and the good of others. I was a statistic, a teen mom, single and barely scraping by.

While operating in my old beliefs, life brought to me pain and turmoil. Temporary separation from reality became a necessary survival technique. This is why I turned to substances. The world had taken my dreams, my fairytales all of my imaginary princes and replaced them with abusers, drunks, druggies, perverts, failure, lack and scarcity. With no hope of a bright future the agenda becomes; numb the pain, steal, cheat, and fight all in the name of survival. When I had reached that point, clouded by the veil of self-preservation, I simply couldn't see that hurting others was hurting myself. Completely disconnected from the spirit my mind decided, it's me vs. the world; the connection or oneness with everything was nonexistent. This took me even further away from my true nature or natural state of being and deeper into suffering.

Everything you give out, you get back. This is the universal law of Karma. If you are giving out fear, anger, and distrust, this is what you will get back. If you are giving out love and joy, peace and happiness, this is what you will get back. Both are stored in the karma bank. Diminishing others, hurting, stealing or gossiping, is like a withdrawal from the karma bank, creating a deficit that you will one day be forced to pay back.

Give what you wish to receive. If you want money you must give money. If you want love, give love. If you want trust, give trust.

Taking on the world at fifteen and having a child a seventeen, I had made a lot of withdrawals from the karma bank. I didn't have anyone around me that had seen or experienced a higher path. The options available were limited by what I knew. Every day I embarked on the classroom of the world, and my teacher was Mr. Hardknocks. Some of the daily lesson plans involved; How to steal, return what you stole for money to buy diapers 101, how to do whatever it takes to keep the lights on and food on the table, even more important how to tune out the gunshots and when to run. Mr. Hardknocks showed me how to survive and I was a very good student! I rationalized stealing from stores with the fact that I wasn't stealing from people, just businesses who could afford it (That was one of Mr. hardknocks favorite sayings). It was easy to feel like a victim while taking care of my son, going to college, and doing my best to take steps to create a good life for us. Feeling like a victim was all it took to enroll in Mr. Hardknocks classes.

How could feeling broken down by a cold cruel world that is against me not occur, when I watched all the other eighteen year olds depicted on television living carefree lives burdened only by making sure they had the latest shoes and designer clothes. My typical day began at 4:30am driving my son to daycare. After dropping him off an hour out of the way, I had just enough time to run, praying I brought the right bag with my homework, to a 6 am speech class. My college classes were only the beginning; I had a barter worked out with the daycare provider. I cooked lunch, fed the kids and put them down for a nap while she went to the casino. This exchange paid for his daycare. Most evenings were spent at the western wear store where I had been working for two years. This job blessed me with the money to afford books for school and some of our living expenses. The owners had allowed me to bring my son to work with me while he still was able to be confined to a bouncy seat.

When my son started crawling it was a sign that I had to find alternatives for his care. With no barters available and the high cost of daycare far out of my budget, I found myself wearing all those labels I had given all of those women that I imagined waiting for their government handout. I was a welfare mom that would never amount to anything. I was everything that I knew I would never be. In an instant I became another number waiting to speak with a case worker and ask for state daycare assistance. I was defeated, frustrated and disgusted.

It didn't take long to realize that state assistance was not enough to live off, no matter how meager your living conditions. I spent countless hours applying and interviewing for a position as a waitress, knowing that I could surpass minimum wage with the tips and maybe get us out of this hell we were currently residing in. Coming to terms with the fact that not being of age to consume, and therefore serve alcohol is frowned upon by the managers hired to find employees for these establishments was inevitable. It wasn't long before I realized my chances of getting a waitressing position at a restaurant without being a blood relative or working my way up, which may take years, were microscopic at best.

"Everyone has inside them a piece of good news. The good news is you don't know how great you can be! How much you can love! What you can accomplish! And what your potential is." Anne Frank

I was raising a baby in a house full of drug addicts. I had

ended up there as a last resort I saw no other options: my parents had disowned me when they discovered my pregnancy. Seeing nowhere else to go, I was forced back in to the arms of my son's father. He grew increasingly abusive and unstable. He would be-little me with names, and threaten suicide if I tried to leave. I found him with a gun to his head on more than one occasion and at times he had threatened to take my life as well as his own. I knew I needed to get my son out of this situation.

It is interesting that from the ages of fifteen to eighteen I endured endless violent outbursts and the straw that broke the camel's back was the morning of my sons first birthday. I was making my sons father breakfast, when he walked down the stairs and sat at the kitchen table. I could feel him staring at me. I looked at him and he had the look of utter disgust on his face. Familiar with this look, I was silently praying I wouldn't say or do the wrong thing.

That was the moment I discovered, there wasn't a right or wrong thing I could do that would change his behavior. I was walking on egg shells and no matter what I did they would crack. He stands up and leans over my shoulder, I could feel his breath on my ear and he says,

"You make me sick! I don't love you and I never have! Everything about you is repulsive!"

Fear instantly set in. Worried he was going to get violent; I apologized and pretended to go to the bathroom. I ran out of the house and down the street to the neighbors. Once safely in their house, I laid on their floor beneath the window sill, afraid he would come by and look through the window and see me motionless until his car passed on the street. Then, I knew he had gone to work and it was safe to go home. I hated myself for staying. My whole family was coming over that evening to celebrate and I didn't want anyone to know. I put on a happy face. By the time my family had arrived he had already begged my forgiveness and told me none of it was true. I knew I needed to get out for the sake of my son.

At the time, my brother, the drug addict, had recently moved to an apartment with his newest girlfriend, her son, and a few other people. He had agreed to let me and my son sleep on the floor in his living room as a temporary solution. However, my brother also had fits of violent rage, and he usually directed them at me. I had thankfully, at this point in my life, experienced this enough to have mastered the art of defusing his attention to allow me time to escape.

Living at my brother's house felt like moving from one hell to another. The only change was the mailing address. A steady stream of troubled people all working under the principles taught by Mr. Hardknocks flowed in and out of the house. They were far less restrictive about who their victims were. Growing up with a drug addict I knew that feeding a habit means, you stop asking the questions like "Who is this going to hurt? Do I really need this?" and you stop at nothing to get the next fix.

Being a young, protective mom, this was a very difficult situation. I just kept telling myself it was temporary. Everyone knew that most of my free time was spent looking for a job and praying to a god I didn't yet believe in, to stop the suffering. I would rock my son to sleep, close my eyes and pray that everything would be all right. Most of all, I prayed that I find the way to get us out of this drug-infested house. Then someone I never would have expected came as a messenger, of what I thought was the answer to my prayers.

Souls who are searching always find the teacher that will bring them their peace of mind

One afternoon while seated at the kitchen table filling out endless job applications Dan, a friend of my brothers, sat down next to me and said, "Hey, I know the manager at this place."

Perfection is the only way I can describe the sound of those words. It didn't matter the source of the words, they were what I had been praying for. Being naïve, optimistic, and up against a wall, I didn't have to think twice. I had hit too many closed doors; if there was an open door I was walking through it! All I needed to know was when and where.

A mother's love can drive her to sacrifice her own happiness for the happiness of her children

Dan and I never discussed the logistics of the job and this hadn't bothered me until the very moment I saw, wrapped in pink neon, a giant horrendously tacky sign that said: "Dejavu Showgirls, 50 beautiful girls and 3 ugly ones." In that moment, any hopes I had about moving up in society and getting out of the hole I had found myself in quickly dissolved. Surely shock and dismay was written all over my face. Sadly enough, this was just the sort of thing that fit into my expectations of life and people. Based on my experiences so far, I wasn't even angry or offended. I was embarrassed that I had once again tricked myself into believing I was more than a commodity.

We got out of the car and started towards the door that once closed would seal off the exit to the underworld, leaving me unable to see my way out. As we entered the doors of hell, debauchery and sleaze seemed to be palpable.

Everywhere I looked there were women who were baring their skin, wearing stiletto heels, excessive makeup, push-up bras and panties. The D.J. announced Mercedes to stage one and Billy Idol gently serenaded me with Cradle of Love. The only light seemed to come from the colorful array of strobe lights on the main stage, the D.J's part in the overall artistic expression of choreography between dancer, music and lights. A mixture of cigarette smoke, hairspray, stale perfume and popcorn brought the final touches to the overall ambiance that reeked of class. We were seated and I was in awe, unable to find words, an uncommon scenario for me. When Dan's friend arrived, he greeted me with "Hey there, darling." I took in a deep breath in an effort to calm the powerfully overwhelming sensation of nausea that rushed through me at the sound of those words. "Could he have been any more predictable?" I thought.

The next half hour was spent with Steve telling me how much money I would make, how happy all of the girls were, and how I could use this as a stepping stone to doing great things in my life...blah...blah...blah. I believe he even used the words "big family" at one point. He explained all of the procedures necessary to get my license and how "my new family" would make it as easy as possible, how I wouldn't have to worry about finding the money for the license as they would happily pay all of my expenses up front because that was how sure they were that I would make big money. The general pitch seemed to consistently pound in the idea that they really just had my best interest at heart.

This is where the filters you see the world through can affect your decisions. Having been raised in an unsupportive environment with a drug addict while suffering from sexual abuse, I had no understanding of boundaries. I was ideal for a guy like this. Birds of a feather flock together, and I was no different from all of the people surrounding, me. I had low self-esteem and a lack of self-worth. My sexual boundaries had already been compromised due to abuse, and I was living in fear, scarcity, and lack. By the time I left the club that evening, I had an appointment to meet Steve at the court house to apply for my business license and a scheduled first day of work.

The ride home was the first time I thought to myself, "Can I even do it?" Even though every cell in my being was shutting down in utter distaste, all of the beliefs that were pressed on me in my youth said this is just how life is…It's not all rainbows and butterflies and often you have to do things you don't want to. Since it was the only path showing up for me clear and visible with all the steps laid, I thought I should just put one foot in front of the other and see where it leads.

My Sacrifice

The agreement I made to start working for Steve was a giant leap into fear, the start to my steady decline. So many people looked down on me in judgment and disgust even I felt I didn't deserve respect because of how I supported myself. What kind of person sells her body for money? But, I know that kind of person intimately, because it was me.
Being a quick learner, I didn't make it too far on my journey into Dante's inferno before I discovered that there was a formula to selling your soul in tiny incremental pieces, and it involved large doses of alcohol and drugs. The drugs were like rose colored glasses: getting high takes the edge off a find life tolerable or at least stop caring. Life turns into something you're watching play out from an outside perspective. When the high wears off, all you are left with is a giant void in the center of your soul and the memories of what you did while you were numb.

Alcohol and drugs are a suppressant of your soul and your spirit. They dim your light and allow the darkness to seep in. The situations I began to find myself in, the decisions and choices I made were all based on information being provided by society's virus. Fear created beliefs that it was me against the world and the world was; fear, lack, scarcity, pain, sorrow, hurt, anger, frustration, and betrayal.

Over the Rainbow

CHAPTER SIX

~Purification~

While looking for that glimmer of light or hope in a world that can through certain lenses seem consumed with darkness you must tune in to the frequency of the light. Light gives life to everything, it is gods' eyes looking upon all the inhabitants of the earth with love. In drugs and alcohol you are living in the dark. The bank of Karma is found in a sacred temple illumined in a vibrant, white light. Even the bank of karmas light can be dimmed by the darkness of drugs making it invisible. Freedom from the chains binding your heart depends on repayment of karma.
The coordinates are only available to a whole being. A body, detached from its mind or spirit can't just wander aimlessly into a karma bank. Your Body, mind and spirit must ask for forgiveness and directions arrive.

For the spirit to see your body as a ripe and fit place to reside and decide to reconnect, the body temple must be pure and cleansed of all toxins. Alcohol, drugs, cigarettes, and processed food must be eliminated and soon a new clarity of mind will bring with it right action, drawing you closer to true happiness and joy.

Creating a place fit for your soul isn't easy. You will have to earn your passage to true happiness by learning a few lessons along the way and dealing directly with your past to find resolutions, forgiveness, and a pure unconditional love for yourself.

Purifying your body temple is a surefire way to rapidly begin illuminating your path to a higher frequency

After clearing your energetic field of all interference, you will begin to make that faithful trek back up the hill. Along the way, you will be asked to pay back everything that you have borrowed from the karma bank. In full faith, you must happily- with no attachment feed the karma bank...with nothing tangible in return.

My Karmic debt consisted of $13,000 in fines and tickets I had received while I was making withdrawals. This was the cost of buying back my soul. If I had a $500 night at work, I got a $500 ticket. Some of the tickets were driving-related, some were fines and fees or bills I forgot I had. I could use the cash to pay my immediate bills like rent, utilities, food to stay afloat, but eventually the karma bank was going to ask for repayment from all the loans.

That 8x8 holding cell was Karma's debt collectors looking for repayment. Bringing valuable lessons and building strength, integrity and character they begin the process of removing the layers clouding the lenses. From my viewpoint a clear picture was being painted of a world that was against me. I had much more in common with all the lowlife's, criminals and vagrants I encountered on a daily basis than I had realized. It seems we had all stumbled into a series of circumstances driven by bad luck that just didn't end. Doors shut when you are living in fear on survival mode and it feels a lot like bad luck. The low vibration says, "Life is hard and the world is against you. You are unlucky. The truth hurts." High vibration sees those situations very differently. Replacing those thoughts with "life is good, everything is always unfolding for the highest and best outcome and the truth reveals the beauty, miracles and magic that is all around you all of the time."

As you raise your vibration through purifying the body, you get glimpses living a life completely immersed in faith and love. Your choices are born of desire, service and infinite possibility, not because life has left you with no other choice. You become a giver, looking for ways to be of service. The low vibration says, "take because there isn't enough; you better get some before it's gone." In high vibration, you will give, searching for nothing in return.

Our biggest lessons are never easy. It is hard to see the good in situations that bring you to your knees in pain and hurt. It is even harder have faith that releasing what little you perceive that you have is precisely what is necessary to allow more to come.

Now, I was at the mercy of the law. Free temporarily but, an innocent jaunt to the grocery store for milk could land me in jail. I had been in every jail in two counties; my son was beginning to think police officers were bad because they kept taking his mommy away. Eventually something snapped. I wanted to take back my power and control. The way out was unclear. Good/ bad and right/wrong become confused in the dark. I acted blindly and decided I was going to get somewhere that I had absolutely no evidence even existed.

Now, I look back and am grateful for the contrast. I needed to find the bottom to decide with an unbreakable conviction I was going to find the top. The bottom inspired me to free myself of the chains that had been binding me. It was the absolute conviction and determination to not have my freedom taken away again that allowed the seal covering the hole to peel back revealing just enough light to show me the way out.

I saw an opportunity to make money in Los Angeles. I packed up my car and drove cross country. I worked endless hours dancing, modeling, movies, commercials anything I could to add to the stash of money I was acquiring. I had been all over the country working as an exotic dancer, and the seedy underworld of Los Angeles was by far the most dangerous. So, knowing my way around a strip club came in handy. Everywhere you turn, someone wants to use you up or get you out, if you are taking theirs.

I am certain I must have worked at every single club in Southern California before finding the one that was the best fit and when I did, it became my home for 24 days that would become a turning point in my life.

The occasional test showed up to see if I was ready. Was I firmly rooted or could I be derailed from my purpose. I had very convincing offers for X-rated magazines and movies, which promised me large sums of money, but I stayed true to my mission. I had seen people take that path and never come back, and I knew I didn't want to be a casualty. The temptation and offers never stopped, but I was unaffected. I picked a medium sized club in Hollywood and made that club more money than it had ever seen. I danced for producers, directors, famous actors, and writers, and called it a day's work. I worked on movie sets and commercials and hobnobbed with the rich and famous. It took about a month to make the money I needed, and at the end of it I was fatigued and broken. Bandaged feet, beaten down, exhausted body and a tattered soul. In my heart I knew it was time.

Keep your eyes open for the signs. They are always there lighting your path.

Knowing I had made what I needed wasn't enough to break the cycle of returning to get more. It would take a sign from above and that sign came one day when two girls I had worked with in Seattle walked into the club looking for a job. Shocked to see someone I knew so far from home, I excitedly let them know I had found a great motel that was clean and inexpensive in Malibu. Leaving them with the motels information I returned to work. On their way out, after filling out the necessary paperwork they got my attention and said "We got a room! We are in #360. Come over when you get off!"

It all happened so suddenly from there. Just thirty minutes later, I was hit by an onset of an extremely violent food-poisoning take down. I left work and spent the entire car ride vomiting into any container I could find. The sheer force of what seemed like endless amounts of vomit spewed from me so violently I spent most of my drive with no choice but to open my car door and lean out. Thankfully the traffic in L.A. rarely hits a speed faster than 25 MPH.

When I finally arrived at my hotel room there was little relief. Hours passed and my condition slowly deteriorated, I had attained a level of delirium where I was certain death was inevitable. Delirium allowed me to transcend reality creating the perfect environment to talk with God...Yes; I often talked with god as a last result. I turned to him, when I felt as though I didn't have anyone else that could hear me. Growing up in a home without religion my god didn't have a face or a name, but always seemed to come through in my darkest hour.

Our conversation began as I lay on the floor of my hotel room. Lying in the midst of vomit and feces, my body depleted of all energy, I mustered the strength to place my hands together in prayer and thank god for giving me all he had. I thanked him for the love of my son and prayed he would take care of him. I felt strangely peaceful, as if it was my time to go. I closed my eyes and as I drifted off god responded. The voice whispered gently in my ear and felt loving and kind. It said, "I sent you help. Remember? It's not your time. Call the girls."

How could I have forgotten the Seattle girls from earlier that day? I had spent a lifetime relying only on myself, so it hadn't even occurred to me to call someone for help. Suddenly I found the will to survive. The will gave me the strength and I made it to the phone. Within minutes I was on my way to the hospital.

The choice is always yours.

The next morning, well on my way to healing, I found myself at a crossroads. That night had been a sign. I knew I had completed what I set out to complete. I had made enough money to pay off my fines and debt and start again, but I had to make a choice between two roads. One road, the higher one, had abundance, prosperity and more than enough to go around for everyone. Below that was the road more often chosen, the road that has signs everywhere saying Beware. On this path there is scarcity and lack, and people are fighting for what little resources there are. For me, the toll for the high road was handing over the $13,000. But the toll for the low road is always the same: your happiness.

It starts with a wish, a prayer, or an intention. "I wish I had $13,000 to dig myself out of debt." The money arrives at your feet. Now, to create and expand into newness, you have to do things differently. The old me would have spent the money on materialistic things, stemming from fear. The new me paid the toll of $13,000 and took the high road. It was the climactic point in my life. I had managed to break the cycle and kept my happiness intact.

Most people find themselves reliving this vicious cycle of scarcity and lack, and, like I did, tell their stories from the context of "poor me." Until we pay back the karma bank, we can't see the doors that are open in front of us.

Paying back the karma bank cleaned the mirror to my soul.

When I paid all of my fines, the gift I received cannot be explained to those who see gain only through materialistic acquisition; it was far greater than anything I could have acquired as a physical possession. Before I paid the toll, it felt as though I had an imaginary chain around my ankle that was adhered to the ground, and I could never make it too far or this chain would pull me back. After I paid, that chain dissolved and I was free.

We all have imaginary chains that hold us back from experiencing life. These chains come from our training, our upbringing, what stories we were told as children, and they are so powerful and they live only in our imagination. In the circus, elephants are trained using this system of imaginary chains. These powerful, robust beasts travel with the circus as it moves from town to town. Circuses have to be very versatile, as they do not have special confines for the animals most of the places they visit. Imagine the kind of cages or chains necessary to stop a determined elephant from running.

Their solution to maintaining control of the elephants without proper equipment or chains begins when the elephants are very small. Before the animal gets too large and strong, it can be easily contained by a shackle and a single chain. The trainer places one end around the baby elephant's ankle and the other end around a pole that has been cemented into the ground. The small elephant will, with an incredible amount of fervor, fight against this chain and try to break free for as long as it physically can. Eventually, the elephant gives up and learns that no matter how hard it tries, it cannot escape, his spirit has been broken. It is in that moment that the elephant no longer needs to be bound. From then on a simple chain around its ankle—one it could easily break as it grows bigger and stronger—is enough to stop the elephant from even attempting to break free.

Paying these fines unlocked the chain from my ankle and I was released. The world opened up! My action came from pure faith, and I could not have known the gift I would get in return until I took the first step.
View opportunities to pay back the karma bank as a blessing. It is just that: an opportunity! Bathe yourself in the light of pure gratitude when repayment is requested, viewing it as a sign that you are learning and growing.

Become acutely aware of any statement that begins with the ever powerful, magical words, "I believe." The words that follow are words you are choosing to live by, so choose carefully! When I am speaking with people and I hear them starting a statement with "I believe," I immediately stop them and have them hear what they said, because knowing your beliefs is the first step towards changing them.

It is crucial right now that you acknowledge any limiting beliefs you have. You have the power to change your world as effortlessly as changing your mind. Although the effort is minimal, the difficulty is high. You have spent a lifetime proving this belief to be true, so you have trained your mind to think, live, see, and feel this belief. Weigh every belief you have on the scale of happiness. One side consists of beliefs filled with optimism, love, happiness, and faith. The other side gets filled with beliefs that keep you bound in a fear, scarcity, lack, judgment, anger, resentment. Your beliefs should knock the scale way off balance leaning to the side of love. If the other side is weighed down with worry, guilt, shame, anger or frustration, choose right now to change that!

You are one of the courageous ones. You are healers, teachers, and leaders, here to make a huge impact on society. You alone can change the way the world is viewed and awaken all of those who are still sleeping, ailing from the virus. You can make the choice.

"Minds are like flowers. They only open when the time is right."
Stephen Richards

The world is full of people who are sleepwalking through their lives, going through the motions with no real passion or purpose. Awakening to your truth, passion and purpose, has revealed your duty to awaken others. Deep down, you have always known you had something special to offer. The world has been waiting for you to emerge into your greatness and you are sitting on the cusp right now.

I encourage you to start looking for answers by asking questions. Wash away the debris clouding your lenses and start to see clearly your true self, your infinite and divine being. One of the layers of fog on your lenses is the media, where a select few use their beliefs as filters to choose what "information" to deliver to the rest of us.   And this information is skewed and biased at best.

Fear sells. It is the heart of the virus. The first step to the cure is to stop accepting things as true just because you read it or saw it on television. The information being displayed as facts builds the reaction they want you to feel, not the feeling that empowers you or adds to your story; cable programming endorses the feeling that brings discord into your body. The media tapers the stories to directly feed the virus. One news story told just right can allow the virus to overpower you, insisting that you watch the whole program; the virus then filters the information throughout all the cells in your body distributing little doses of fear into your operating system. Since the virus attaches itself to fear and craves more fear to feed on, you can easily start to experience reasons to be fearful everywhere you go. Soon, fear is clouding the lenses you view the world through.

The debris on your lenses has accumulated over your lifetime. Taking control of what you allow into your conscious and subconscious mind will eventually clear the virus from your cells. Without food it can't survive. Without the virus controlling the way you see the world, the world opens up. It will be unveiled as a series of truths, each veil removed and a truth revealed, as you are ready to accept them. Be aware that the world will look different when the veils are removed. You will need to remind yourself often of the commitment to be a good student with an open mind. Be willing to receive this new world exactly as it arrives.

It takes courage and strength to see things as they are, to live with integrity as these things are revealed. With all growth, great rewards will come. Your passion and purpose will be revealed to you as you connect on a deeper level with your higher self, your true self. As you live on purpose, life will flow with ease and grace and, as quickly as the thought arrives, you will begin to manifest things into your life that serve your higher purpose.

How do you remove the veils of illusion and begin to see things through the pure, untainted eyes of a child?

Try closing your eyes and then opening them again. Does everything that you see get lost in insignificance because you have seen it all before? Do you notice only what's out of place or different? Can you pretend you are seeing it all for the first time? If you were to look around and allow your mind to process as it always does, your mind will place labels on everything it sees and the object will then lose its magic. It becomes familiar and safe. Instead, see it like you did when you were young, before the stories changed things. View the world with curiosity and amazement. Remove the labels, clear your mind, and view your surroundings with intrigue. Notice the stories that you tell yourself as you look at things. Try looking at objects or scenes around you and describe how these objects make you feel. To be fully awake, you must master the art of presence. Feel, smell and see all that surrounds you in any given moment.

All we ever have is this one breath. Don't waste it in fear, haste, anger or judgment. Let every breath be an opportunity to be in love, peace, joy and happiness.

Don't let life pass you by, filing everything away under "familiar and safe" and rarely venturing out into the unknown filled with curiosity, anticipation and amazement. All you ever really have is this moment, this breath. Be eternally grateful each day as your eyes open, for no other reason than the fact that you woke up! You now have this day to fill with pure greatness. Not everyone will wake up today, and the ones that don't may have regrets, wishing they had taken chances, loved more, or given more. On the wall in my bedroom is a scroll with a prayer from the Dalai Lama embroidered on it.

The first few lines of the prayer are…

"A Precious Human Life: everyday think as you wake up, today I am fortunate to have woken up, I am alive, I have a precious human life, I am not going to waste it." Dalai Lama

What a powerful way to wake up, find gratitude, and set your intention for the day. The uncertainty of the future leaves the mind with too much room, and that room is often thoughtlessly fill with worries, fears, and concerns. The mind gets wound up in its spiraling tales of what ifs and why not's, and before you know it the moment is lost. As children, being present was a natural state.

I knew I wanted that again. For the sake of my growth, I wanted to travel to my childhood home and look at it as though for the first time. I wanted to go back to before and find freedom from all the burdens of adulthood, to travel through time and access that place in my mind when the unknown was still a mysterious, magical wonderland of possibilities, the place that existed before I accepted other stories about what is.

"We are shaped by our thoughts; we become what we think. When the mind is pure, joy follows like a shadow that never leaves."
Guatama Buddha

Typically pictures or painting's we see depicting childhood bring a sense of joy and happiness. For me, Norman Rockwell captures that essence perfectly. His pictures don't show a search for happiness or a discovery of happiness; they depict an experience that just expects happiness. Looking at his pictures sparks something in my soul that speaks of joy. I wondered if this innocence was ever a part of me. If everything I now believe is inspired by my past, what would it look like without my past to corrupt its perfection? I had held the pure essence of happiness and joy in my hands, too, at some point. I wanted to remember and see life from that place.

So many veils of illusion have been placed over that purity, veils accumulated throughout life, causing distortion of the world you see around you. Illusions come from accepting the thoughts and beliefs of others without questioning their value to you. You must begin to lift these veils and reveal your truth, to connect to your higher purpose. Discover who you really are and you will discover your happiness and joy again.

Over the Rainbow

CHAPTER SEVEN

~Lifting the Veils of Illusion
Seeing Your Truth~

You and I are infinite beings. Even though we are often unaware of our connection, we are never separated from the divine will. When we recognize this unbreakable bond, we discover that we are creators of our destiny. Divine will, has a purpose intended just for you, a contribution you were specially designed to make. Tuning in, is remembering who you are free of all the labels.

Without labels, the world can be seen through eyes of innocence and will return to its truest form. This form has no hate, fear, anger, disease. Instead, it is filled with the divine nature of happiness, joy and infinite creation. You are standing in the midst of this perfect world right now; the only things that keep you from experiencing it are the screens between you and what is real. It has taken a lifetime to develop these screens of fear, scarcity, and painful memories that act as a filter for truth and separate you from divine will and your purpose.

Children cause our filters to drop away and allow us to see purity and innocence. They haven't set up their screens of delusion or distorted their perception with beliefs yet. But for many of us, how we see adults —merely these children grown up — is distorted by our perceptions and experiences in life.

Imagine a picture of two people holding hands on the beach and gazing into one another's eyes, the sun illuminating the water as it sets. This shows a captured moment of romance and happiness, but it might not hold the authentic feeling-tone of true, untainted bliss. Why? This picture is someone's arrival at a happy place, leaving you to create the story of what they might have gone through to get there. What each of us sees is very biased, skewed by our story. If you have always been abused by your lovers, and they would bring flowers and love letters of apology after, you may look at this picture and see pain, not joy. It is imperative on your path to self-discovery that you begin by recognizing your stories. What are yours?

"...a child does not have to be taught how to be happy or the ways of love. It is fear, hatred and prejudice that have to be taught. And from the condition of the world we can see that, unfortunately, there are some pretty good teachers." Javan

Childhood was that time for me, when I was wide open to love, happiness and joy. I didn't have stories running around my head, ready to insert into any situation and fill in the blanks. I saw everything at face value. I returned to my childhood home as an experiment. I had heard someone say, "It was so much easier in those days, the days when we didn't have to worry about car payments, mortgage, job, relationships etc." I wanted to see if I could remember what it felt like to be free of all of those burdens. Almost as quickly as I arrived in front of the house, I felt my chest contract and my breath become shallow. I began to feel my adrenal glands kicking in and my fight or flight instinct saying "run as far as you can! Never look back!"

"My journey into the canyon began and the terrain was rough. With so many scratches and bruises, I had to numb the pain..."

As a teenager, I still had no memory of the abuse that had happened in my home. Then, one life-altering afternoon, I was lying in my dad's recliner in agonizing pain. My menstrual cycles as a young teen had become almost too painful to bear. Sometimes I would lie on the bathroom floor and pray for death rather than suffer for one more minute. For one week every month, the thought of killing myself and end the pain was actually soothing.

I now know this was all preparation. Dealing with that kind of pain, you learn to find peace in the most uncomfortable circumstances able to stay centered and grounded. You learn to accept what you cannot change. I didn't know it then, but I was mastering the ability to separate from my physical body and connect with a higher realm. I had used this technique when I was little as a means to separate from the abuse I was experiencing, so this mastery was the result of the years I had spent in preparation.

On that particular afternoon: As a way to try to ignore the excruciating pain, I decided to use up the one-hour-per-day of TV time, allotted by my father. I turned on an afternoon special about a girl who was being sexually abused by a neighbor.

"Poor thing" I thought, empathizing with her story. When a strange thing happened: like a nuclear explosion, my head began to buzz as if bees were swarming around me. My throat tightened and the air suddenly lacked sufficient oxygen. My own skin felt foreign, unfamiliar, and I had to get away from it. I jumped out of the chair I and ran as fast as I could to my room.

By the time I had launched myself past the threshold of my bedroom door and onto the bed, I was panic-stricken. All of the signs of pure terror were present, my heart was racing, my breathing was hindered and my skin was crawling. Unsure what was happening, I pulled out my journal and a pen from the night stand and started writing.

Memories flashed through my head and my fingers, grasping the pen with knowingness beyond my understanding, began moving across each line, filling page after page, struggling to keep up with the memories. Fighting through cramping fingers and clenched jaw, I couldn't stop.

When I was done I looked at the notepad in front of me, a notepad my Grandma had given me the Christmas before. The front cover read, "Shoot for the moon and you will fall among the stars." Now the lines on the pages were filled in, not with typical middle school stories of who I liked or who I dreamed would ask me to the upcoming dance. On those pages I had written detailed descriptions of years of abuse that, until that very moment, had been locked somewhere deep in my subconscious.

I had to make a choice: lock the notebook back in my drawer and the memories back in my subconscious…or tell someone. The possible outcomes of telling someone; at least the possibilities I could see through the eyes of adolescence, all ended with my life crumbling to pieces. The decision became clear. Put the memories back where they came from and pray they stay there this time.

What I didn't realize then was the irrevocable damage that moment of divinely-inspired recollection had placed on my path. Keeping my newly-gained memories locked in my subconscious would prove to be eminent doom, requiring synthetic pain relief just to mute the voices. My prayers were answered when marijuana was bestowed upon me by my brother at the age of thirteen.

Even the most harmless of medicines have an endless list of possible side effects cascading down the side of the bottle. Our society places little regard on the side effects deciding in most cases, the benefit outweighs the risk. Outweighing the risks of Marijuana for me was the much needed time to mature and gain enough strength to take on the process of healing.

Eventually Marijuana wasn't enough for the job. As the pain increased so did the strength of the drug. Like every other statistic, or lost soul, I stopped reading the side effects and started taking into my body anything I could get my hands on. By the age of 20 I had experimented with cocaine, acid, ecstasy, ice, meth, alcohol, muscle relaxers, pain killers and more.

Opportunities to grow stronger are what life is all about. We just need to make sure that are backs are strong enough to endure the weight.

I was lost and in search of a greater meaning to life. I didn't know what love looked like but I knew it felt good to get attention and the feeling I received from the sound of the words "I love you" was worth enduring. My first real boyfriend would be the template for many more to come. At fifteen I was kicked out of my home. I spent several months bouncing from one friends couch to another until I finally landed on my boyfriend's couch.

I didn't know all of the different ways that love and happiness could look. I only knew what my experience had showed me. I couldn't even entertain the possibility of a "nice guy." Instead I favored of the guys who had a tendency towards violence, mental and physical abuse. I was programmed to be a victim in silence as my lips were still sealed about the abuse I had suffered as a child. My relationship with this boyfriend was my first opportunity for inner growth. I did find the strength to leave him eventually, but not before we were permanently bound together for life.

Just two months after leaving him, I realized the flu I thought I had was actually the bestowing of a beautiful blessing. At seventeen I was pregnant.

The universe gave me the gift of discovering true love in the eyes of my son.

Pregnancy was my strength. I temporarily stopped drinking, smoking cigarettes and marijuana, and started taking prenatal pills. Purifying my body was easy when it was for the health and well-being of my unborn baby. I quickly transitioned from being a child to becoming a child in charge of me, plus one. I had school, an apartment, a job, and a baby. I didn't have time to place the pieces in the right spots; I just needed to finish the puzzle as soon as possible.

I had never been shown a love that was compassionate, kind and caring, I had absolutely no reference to even experience that and call it love. The love I knew was despondent and cold, and taken away just as easily as it was given. Although my heart had been wounded and callused, even bitter and defeated everything changed the moment my son was placed in my arms. My son melted away all the layers covering it and rewrote my program entitled "love."

Daydream Your Life into Reality!

"What if you slept? And what if, in your sleep, you went to heaven and there plucked a strange and beautiful flower? And what if, when you awoke, you had the flower in your hand? Ah, what then?" Samuel Taylor Coleridge

During those early adolescent years, I spent most of my free time daydreaming myself into a new place, a habit I have held onto for my entire life. With a wild imagination and the idea that anything is possible—topped with a hint of stubbornness—I infused these dreams with creativity and was determined to make them real one day. I would spend hours dreaming about the day freedom would find me and like Rapunzel I would be released from the confines of the castle walls. Romanticizing the idea of packing a bag and venturing out into the world that I had seen displayed on that magical box, the television and in magazines.

I envisioned a fantasy world where people loved one another and were kind, caring and happy. Reading books was a beautiful escape technique that sharpened my skills as a dreamer. It allowed my mind to separate from what my senses told me was true and expand outside of those current circumstances, creating infinite possibilities. Books gave me the kind of hope that can only be found in your own imagination. They gave me hopes of being whisked away to a castle, by my knight in shining armor. It had happened for Cinderella; it could happen for me! He would marry me and make me a princess. My Romeo would be the picture of pure perfection. Books showed me there might be more.

"Imagination is more important than knowledge. For knowledge is limited to all we now know and understand, while imagination embraces the entire world, and all there ever will be to know and understand." ~ Albert Einstein

So what stopped me from making my dreams a reality? Why wasn't I being rescued by a prince? I was always told how beautiful I was. I was told that I could have any man I wanted. This was true to a point: I would always successfully get the guy that everyone wanted. The problem was, in my world, "everyone" was not saying much! Having grown up with dysfunction, abuse, and an addict brother, I always managed to find someone who fit right into my area of expertise. My problem was not getting the guy. My problem was that even the best abusive and angry alcoholic really isn't a win!

As I had become more connected to my higher purpose and the veils were lifted, I began to see things as they were for people outside of my immediate surroundings. I saw people in healthy, loving relationships. I saw that I wasn't really a victim of circumstance, but that life can only reveal to you what your expectations are. I needed to raise the bar!

CHAPTER EIGHT

~Angels Really Do Exist~

As the veils lift and your higher purpose becomes clear, your expectations grow too.

To raise the bar I had to understand the veil through which I had been viewing life. If I could remove that belief from my operating system, it would allow me to replace it with a new belief that could broaden my expectations.

When the student is ready the teacher always arrives.

I was ready, just like you are. There are angels everywhere, just waiting to bestow miracles on you. Those angels visited me often, showing up in all different forms. They saw a child carrying a child and offered me assistance or a kind word. They saw the despair on my face and offered me a hug or a genuine smile. In their own way, they were begging me to surrender my worries and concerns to them. They offered to take on the weight of my burdens just long enough for me to regain my strength.

These angels are all around you, too. Yes, those dutiful little busy bodies buzzing all around you are wishing for nothing more than to have you ask for help so they can swoop in and grant your wish. All around you are unsung heroes, guardians of love and the truth. They are seekers, guides, dreamers and believers who understand the magical elements of pure, unconditional love that society has forgotten. These angels, disguised as friends, family, or even a passing stranger, will with a moment's notice inherit super powers as they pull out their halo and reveal their wings. They will fly through the turbulent winds of the most devastating storms and dive deep into the seas of despair to show you the way out, and they will never ask for anything but your smile in return.

They hear your plea in the darkest hour and they bring the light. Just cast your prayer to the stars, light your inner spark with a touch of hope, and wait patiently for the whispers, the gentle reminders that it will all be ok. Hope illuminates the soul and deflects fear, allowing your heart to shine like a beacon so the angels can find you in the darkness.

The angel of hope always arrived in the nick of time. When she found me, she whispered poetic, heartfelt words of faith, fearlessness, and triumph in my ear. She reminded me of my strength and power. She told me to do today instead of regret tomorrow. She was always there, urging me to put one foot in front of the other, even without a clear destination.

As the angel of hope guided me toward the idea of a brighter reality, the angel of love appeared to greet me. This angel took my hand and reminded me that all I am is love. In a touch and a glance, I felt the sensation of being cherished and adored. She was the gentle reminder in the form of a phone call, email, or card that reminded me: "I am important and I matter to somebody."

The angel of love opened my heart guided me to the angel of assistance, who always seemed to keep me at the edge of my seat. This angel liked to wait until the last second, when everything was held together by a single thread, to deliver whatever resources I needed to keep me going just one more day.

If you can find a glimmer of light on even the darkest of days, your angel will see your light and come to your aid.

And when you find yourself basking in the beauty and the love that surrounds you, that is the time to look for another beacon of light shining through the dark, because someone else is counting on you to show up for them and be their angel!

No act of goodwill goes forgotten or unnoticed, especially when it is pure of heart. Even the smallest gestures with just the right timing gave me the strength to keep going. Never underestimate your power to heal or help.

How to summon your angels through the power of request:

Write love letters to people who aren't in your life yet. Pretend you are writing to your angels. I write love letters to feel my heart open with love pouring from the deepest part of my soul, as I imagine and visualize the kind of people I want to have near me. I write with a full heart of gratitude to guides, teachers, or higher beings. I write to my angels when I am in search of assistance or to lovers when I want to hold someone's hand. These letters never go unanswered…although the answer isn't always the one I thought it would be!

Your teachers are everywhere. You must be willing to ask for guidance and to always move through life as student with an empty glass, ready to be filled.

I realized as long as I was a good student in search of answers and divine knowledge, the answers always arrived. The truth is the answers can't come until you ask the questions. When asking the difficult questions know that the search for answers and quest for the truth doesn't just benefit you; it is as far from selfish as it can be! Always remember that others are searching, too, and they are relying on you to share your answers. You are somebody's teacher; they have written their letter and are awaiting your response.

There is a parable that speaks of a guru holding his disciple's head under water. The disciple is struggling to be free, desperate for a breath. The guru finally releases the disciple and tells him, "When you want enlightenment as much as you wanted that breath, you will have it just as quickly." In that statement, if you replace the word "enlightenment" with whatever it is, you want desire or wish for, and then you will know how to proceed: when you want whatever you want as badly as you want that next breath, it will be.

It is possible to move so far away from your divine purpose that the creative forces of will and spirit pull your foundation out from under you? Immersed in desperation, fear and despair you just like the disciple passionately desire your dreams and want them as badly as you want that next breath. Your guides are always there for you, revealing your path so clearly that if your eyes and ears are open you won't be able to miss it.

Every time you ask, the answer will arrive. You just have to quiet your mind so you can hear the whispers in your heart

CHAPTER NINE

~The Answers~

*Buddha said, "I do not believe in a fate that falls on men
however they act, but I do believe in a fate that falls on men
unless they act."*

My answers had started to arrive in my mid-20s. I had
realized that I couldn't keep looking at the same problems,
seeing the same people, and doing the same things and
expect to get different answers. I began expanding my
comfort zone and meeting new people, trying new things,
traveling to new places and exploring new possibilities. As I
saw and experienced possibilities that seemed to materialize
out of nowhere—and had definitely never been in my realm
of awareness before—my life began to drastically change.
My career choice changed and new friendships were
established.

*"Every leaf that grows will tell you: what you sow will bear fruit.
So if you have any sense, my friend, don't plant anything but
Love." Rumi*

A lot of people stay where they have established roots
for their entire life, both literally by staying in the same
physical area, and figuratively by staying in the same
mindset. Now is the time to plant new seeds. Seeds are little
intentions you cast out into the wind, intentions that hold
the desires of a new essence your soul needs to flourish.
Maybe you have grown so big that the buildings or people
around you are suffocating your roots, shading you from
your sun. It is time to move if you want to continue to grow
and expand! If you are in need of more light or more space,

a different culture, or anything else, your seed of intention will land in the perfect place to grow and receive proper nourishment, eventually growing strong enough for you to uproot your tree.

In my early 20s I had sent out a seed for growth and freedom. Wanting security and a better lifestyle for myself and my son, I began to search out ways to remain as healthy and vibrant as possible. This was when I stumbled upon yoga and meditation.

In yoga, it is very common to hear teachers repeat the mantra "Worship your body temple." One of my first teachers announced to the class—in an apologetic tone that had a hint of sarcasm— "I should inform you all that a side effect of regular yoga practice is to begin to be more aware of the foods you put into your body and to start to make more healthful choices. Yes, I am sorry to say that soon you will not be able to stop at McDonald's and pick up dinner." Each of the teachers I encountered on my path planted intentions. I had infinite opportunities to either nourish them, inspiring them to grow, or to let them wither and die. Once the seeds had been planted the choice was easy and natural. Just like a tree grows towards the sun, I was drawn to the light.

Nourishment came in the form of yoga and meditation and with continued practice, the seeds began to sprout into a world filled with beauty, happiness, and joy. To keep the garden healthy and vibrant it was in constant need of tending. Weeds can grow in the absence of light and could with ease, strangle and shade my joy from blossoming. The weeds that grow from anger, resentment, frustration, and revenge aren't always easy to let go of; I had spent years watching them grow uncontrollably, even feeding and assisting their growth, naively confusing them with flowers and all the while hindering the ability for dreams, aspirations and joy to come into full fruition. To ensure they wouldn't return, I had to pull them from their roots. The root is found at the weeds conception. Weeds are beliefs established that are untruths.

Letting go is never easy, but if change is what you want then letting go is always necessary. When you start to tend to your garden and cultivate your seeds, you find a new awareness of your body. Cleansing your body of weeds that, left unnoticed, will one day form disease, will deepen your connection to your true state of health and wellness.

Begin to worship the body temple as it is the vehicle that we will use to expand into more of your true self this lifetime.

As veils are lifted, you will discover a renewed sense of clarity as to the worth of your body and the need to treat it with love and respect. It is the vehicle with which you move through life. Think instead about your car: you likely take care in washing your car and would never place anything other than gas into the gas tank. We may have several cars throughout a lifetime, but we get only one body. When we are operating under delusion or veils, we disconnect from our body. We forget that our bodies are incredible machines, designed to heal and renew. We expect things like sickness and disease to ravage our bodies and we feel defenseless to these microscopic organisms. The human condition has accepted sickness as a way of life. This belief is a veil fogging your vision from the truth: that sickness is not a natural condition of the body, but a human condition of the body. If you accept the fundamental viewpoint that you are a "spiritual being having a human experience" and understand that you are spirit living in body, then you will know that spirit cannot be touched by disease or toxins as long as you stay connected in consciousness.

Create the picture of the cells in your body as vibrant, buoyant; illuminated springs that, in their natural state, are expansive, bouncy and open, in this state they are immune to disease and sickness. As we move through life and get caught up in the thoughts that run uncontrollably through the mind, we lose touch with our natural state of spirit. This state needs silence to manifest. For many of us, the thoughts that cloud the mind are unpleasant, perhaps reminiscent of something that has already happened or fearful about what is yet to come. These fear-based thoughts cause the cells of the body to begin to retract and coil up, diminishing their ability to heal. When this happens, the light turns to darkness and the body becomes susceptible to sickness and disease. The doctors call this stress, and it is now considered the number one cause of death. It leads to disease, obesity, migraines and discomfort.

As you travel along this path towards healing your body, you may have moments of clarity that rock your world and change it forever. For me, one of the moments that brought me to tears was the day I decided to never eat meat again.

I have always been what I considered a compassionate human being who has tried to be aware of suffering amongst the plant and animal kingdoms and minimize my part in it. I had always purchased organic meat that had been treated somewhat humanely and not pumped full of antibiotics. I watched the movies about the terrible conditions under which our food animals are farmed and raised, but I watched unconsciously. It wasn't until I requested that the veils be lifted and assured the universe I was ready that I was able to finally see.

I was in a local health-conscious market, alive with

health-conscious earth lovers. This store was my favorite place to buy meat, as they were careful to assure that the animals were raised in humane conditions. This day, was the day that everything changed. I walked up to the cooler that displayed meat, but instead of seeing dinner, I saw flesh on display. I saw birds murdered, plucked, and skinned. I saw animals stripped of their precious lives and put in a cooler with a price tag, with no respect for the animal that gave its life to feed us. Tears streamed down my cheeks and I was shocked by my ability to live blindly for so long. From that day on I have been unable to eat any meat at all. This wasn't easy: my family and boyfriend, unable to understand my newfound vegetarianism, chastised me. But I remain to this day a vegetarian.

The more I continued to remove toxins from my body through yoga and clean eating, the more I could hear what my body needed. Through stillness, I discovered that I no longer wanted substances to numb or distract myself. I was ready to stand before the fears and painful memories embedded deep within me, ready to be clear of mind-altering substances so I could reconnect with my inner guidance and intuition.

I noticed energy shifts in my body as I changed my surroundings or the people I was around. Our senses are designed to work with our inner guidance and intuition like a tuning fork. When I was in a healthy environment surrounded by high vibrations, good people with good intentions, I felt good. The opposite was true as well. The energy I surrounded myself with became just as important as the energy I put into myself.

We are all energetic beings and, like the animals with which we share this planet, we are designed to feel the shift in the earth, to sense the earthquake before it happens

We have created an imaginary separation, infiltrated with the idea that there is a you and a me, a this and a that. This idea of separation only creates dis-ease. Along with the discovery that we are in charge of choosing our thoughts comes the revelation that we should only choose thoughts that serve us or allow us to feel good. When I realized how connected everyone and every living thing is, I was able to connect with a sense of peace and serenity I had never experienced before. I noticed it in small ways first, such as when I thought of someone and then they called, or when I felt drawn to call someone and they said, "I was just thinking about you, how weird that you called."

Animals have not desensitized their ability to feel communication from the world around them. It is a necessary tool for their survival, so they haven't put it to rest. Using their sixth sense, animals have the ability to sense danger before it arrives. They have heightened senses, able to smell or hear things miles away. Animals intuitively move away from danger. They don't prepare for an imagined fate, embracing fear or worry. They respond only to what is. This is what we need to practice again.

We are, by nature, just like the animals. Our ancient ancestors had fine-tuned their sixth sense, viewing themselves as one with the earth that provided a home for crops that in turn sustained life. Today, we humans have come to rely on receiving information from the media or verbal communication, and have tuned out our sixth sense. Reestablishing that connection to the earth is crucial for us in these times, perhaps a matter of life or death for both mother earth and all of the plant and animal species she supports.

"....all things share the same breath....the beast, the tree, the

man....the air shares its spirit with all the life it supports."Chief Seattle -Dwamish

In our lifetime, major natural disasters claim the lives of thousands of humans every year. In 2004, tsunamis struck Africa and Asia. Animals of all different species—monkeys, elephants, and leopards—ran to higher ground, saving themselves. A report quoted the manager of one of the national parks devastated by the tsunami as saying. "We have not found one single animal dead although more than 3000 people were killed." All the animals in his care had gone high into the hills and not returned. According to National Magazine, thousands of people died along India's Cuddalore coast while buffalos, goats, and dogs avoided the disaster. Flamingos that breed that time of year at actually flew to higher ground before the disaster hit.

This seems to show that, had we also been tuned into the changes in the Earth's frequency, we might have had ample time to move to higher ground and be safe. But with our busy minds and no connection to our hearts, we remain separate from the earth and unable to hear her warnings of what is coming.

We are just as capable as animals are of this telepathic connection to the earth. It is as easy as recalibrating a tuning fork. You just need to start tuning into the earth's frequency. As you begin to shift your frequency, you will become much more sensitive to the energy of people and places.

Learn to connect with and trust your energy. It will be your guide.

So how do we connect with our true natures, with spirit? It is crucial that you remain present to the actual experience you are having, as well as find time to allow the mind to be still. Clear the mind, feel the breath, and discover the miracle life has given you. Yoga is one tool that fosters an experience that reunites you with your body, mind, and spirit, making miraculous healing attainable.

Are you prepared to really see life for the first time? Are you ready to lift the veils of illusion distorting your vision?

You should know that it will not be easy. Life as you know it will change as truths are revealed. Traveling on the path of growth and awareness requires you to take action. You will see with clarity, perhaps for the first time, what you are placing in your body, and you will no longer have the urge to place toxins or poisons into your temple, the house of your soul. Fast food, chemicals, and foods packed with preservatives will no longer be an option and you will begin to find time to research how your food is grown and processed. You will, perhaps for the first time, be aware of your spirit, your purpose, the contribution you are here to make.

Acknowledging your body as the home of your spirit, you will make the choice to let your light shine as bright as it can. You will see how much the world needs you. So before you ask to see the world without screens, I urge you to be sure you are really ready. For once your lenses are clear; you will not be able to go back to walking through life with a veil over your eyes.

The world is waiting for who you are becoming.

I have spent many evenings feeling alone even as I stood in a room full of people, as though the whole world were asleep and I was the only one awake. I have found myself compromising my newfound discoveries, thoughts, and beliefs just to fit in with society. Be aware that this may happen as you restructure your world. You can tell your friends what you have discovered, but they may look at you as though you are crazy and ask if you are taking your medications. Understand that spiritual growth can mean that you may not be able to relate to your friends the same way. It can feel as though you no longer belong anywhere.

As I became more sensitive to energy, the people and places that I wanted to be around were affected as well. If one of my friends came by or I bumped into them on the street, I could feel the energy shift in my body. This shift was not always good. Sometimes I would suddenly feel heavy, or my heart rate would increase. I would leave the encounter feeling drained. I didn't know what it was, but I knew I didn't like it. So if I noticed a pattern of being drained every time I was around a certain person or place, I would make a conscious choice to minimize my contact.

It is important as you connect to your higher purpose to honor your energy. You must be aware of who is willing to receive and wanting to grow with you and who wants to pull you back down to a lower vibration. For what has happened is this: you have discovered a new world right here where you are standing. You have dissolved from your consciousness the existence of any negativity, only able to see the beauty all around.

Spirituality isn't for the weak. But, before you put the book down and run away, hear this... if you choose this new clarity, it will change your entire life to one of constant peace, joy, and the purest, truest love.

Over the Rainbow

CHAPTER TEN

~Raise Your Vibration and Your World Changes~

"Form is emptiness; emptiness is form. Form is not different than emptiness; emptiness is not different than form"
PrajnaParamitaHrdaya (The heart sutra)

The world around us consists mostly of space and emptiness. We think we see and feel solid mass, but it is just an illusion. What we actually see is energy vibrating at such an incredible speed that it creates the appearance of a solid mass.

If you took all of the particles of the universe and removed all of the empty space, the entire universe could be shrunk down to a solid mass smaller than a bowling ball. It's an amazing thing to think about, that most of what holds our universe together is, in fact, energy.

"Energy cannot be created or destroyed; it can only be changed from one form to another." Einstein

Everything is energy. Every one of us is energy vibrating on a particular frequency. And just when we tune a radio dial, we can only tune in to one station at a time. Imagine that we all start at conception tuned into smooth jazz. Soon after conception, we begin to pick up our mother's frequency. If she is tuned into a rock station filled with harsh sounds and words, the vibration of your cells begin to mimic the vibration of your mother's cells. Discord soon sets in as you notice, the rock station she is tuned into is vibrating at a low frequency and doesn't resonate well with the body's natural frequency of smooth jazz. In the lower frequencies (or the rock station in this example) fear, hate, anger, guilt, greed are the primary emotions. A good way to detect what you are tuned into is to notice if you are experiencing any of those low vibration feelings. If so, recalibrate or re-tune your radio.

The only way for you to change your experience is to tune your dial into something else. Your emotions and thoughts are the quickest, easiest way to change your radio dial. Begin to think happier thoughts. Do things that tend to cultivate a sense of overall happiness and well-being. Take time to find silence and rediscover the breath. In the silence, let go of ideas you hold onto about how things should be. Notice thoughts of judgment and instantly release them instead of feeding them.

"You are a creature of divine love, connected at all times to source. Divine love is when you see love in everything and everyone you encounter." Wayne Dyer

You were born as pure essence of true love. Even if you don't feel it at this moment, your heart tells you there is more. If you are reading this book, you have followed your heart and began to tune your dial to higher frequencies. You want to have an impact on the planet and be of service to others as they venture onto the turbulent path of truth, leading to the destination of dreams, miracles, happiness, love and whimsical wonder while in awe of all natures' creations.

How do we change our frequency?

Birds of a feather flock together,
And so will pigs and swine;
Rats and mice will have their choice,

and so will I have mine.

- "Birds of a Feather," Nursery Rhyme

As small children, we don't have a lot of control over our frequency. We are at the mercy of whatever frequency emanates in our home or surrounding areas. As we grow older, we step out of what we have been shown and known up until that point, allowing more frequencies to become available to us.

Tuning into a different frequency, will take you to new places, allow you to do new things and connect you with new people. This is the easy part. For most, the difficulty lies in releasing the old people, places, and things that no longer serve your new frequency. Old friends will sense that you are changing and moving on, and they will not want to let you go. Their conscious mind will rationalize the struggle and discomfort present in their subconscious. Resisting the natural urge to flow and move along the current of life will cause disharmony in the subconscious. Since they have forgotten that all disharmonies originate from within not from external circumstances, they look for something to place the blame on; you become the target. Watching you ascend to higher ground makes their stagnancy even more apparent. They will hold on and unaware, they may use low vibration tactics to hold you back. In stagnancy the only tactics available to them will be low vibration such as guilt or shame. You must rise above remaining strong and determined!

My childhood home housed a very low vibration, a vibration I carried with me and viewed the world through for a substantial part of my life. My parents had suffered abuse as children and hadn't discovered the truth that all along there was a whole world, filled with happiness, right under their nose. They stayed stagnant as if they were caught in a special concoction of quicksand; a mixture of fear, pain and distrust. As a child, I inadvertently tuned into all of their frequencies: addiction, low self-esteem and abuse infiltrated my operating system. Although I lived in an upper middle class area, the kind of neighborhood where moms joined the PTSA and girl scouts, they took their daughters to gymnastics and ballet; I saw only the things that followed the frequency set by my parents. Everywhere I looked I saw abuse, distrust, fear, anger and disappointment.

"Strength does not come from physical capacity. It comes from an indomitable will." Mahatma Gandhi

When I escaped my childhood home and had my first child, I knew true love for the first time. Through this, I could now recognize that what my son's father and I shared stemmed from fear and low self-esteem. It was born of the opposite side of the spectrum and lacked a foundation of love. I knew I needed to redefine love.

Our experiences create our definition of love and often love can show up early on in our lives disguised as hurt and pain at the hand of someone you trust and rely on. A fundamental understanding of love is necessary and it begins with a foundation removed of all hurt and pain. Love is an open, trusting, caring, compassionate, safe and vulnerable heart. Most of our path, from birth to death, is discovering and rediscovering love, our true nature. Love is what we are all made of. Even if I didn't quite know how to love myself at that point in my life, I did know how to love my son. He was my guide out of a bad situation and into redefining love.

My son's father embracing the older less refined

definition of love, laid a foundation of fear and complete seclusion from everything I knew. When I was eighteen we bought a house with some money generously gifted from a malpractice suit that had left him permanently disfigured.

We purchased a five acre parcel that sat at the end of a two mile dirt road. On the land was a half built house awaiting endless hours of blood, sweat and tears before it was suitable and safe for a baby. Soon after moving into our new home I discovered that no matter how far away I moved from my old life I couldn't escape it. I would often find myself running from my son's dad just as I used to from my brothers. It was as if my brothers had only been doing me a favor all those years by training me how to hide. I eventually decided that even if I was willing to put up with the abuse, I was not going to allow my son to carry on the tradition. I packed everything I could fit in my car and left behind everything else, like a down payment on my son's and my future happiness.

Even though I had taken this step, I still had many beliefs to change and many veils clouding my perceptions. I continued to be intrinsically drawn to the same types of relationships and people, and they were drawn to me. I didn't know anything else. Everywhere I went, all I saw, felt, or experienced were low vibrations which brought me exactly what I expected: drugs, crime, abuse, guilt, shame, anger and lack.

You choose your reality. Look around you right now. Is this really what you want create? If not, start changing what you see by changing what you think.
The truth is, I didn't know how to make different choices. I had stopped daydreaming and believing in fairytales and had accepted this horror as my reality, unable to see or feel anything other than the frequency I was used to. It wasn't

until later that I discovered I had the ability to retune my radio, that I could choose to change my radio station and watch heaven reveal itself to me right here on earth.

CHAPTER ELEVEN

~Raising your Vibration with Love~
"The hunger for love is much more difficult to remove than the hunger for bread." Mother Teresa

Life had taught me how to protect my heart, never allowing it to be vulnerable or exposed. I was closed off to that heart-on-your-sleeve, fearless kind of love I watched on the big screen. I loved, but in a way that would protect my heart from hurt. When my son was born, my heart became vulnerable and exposed for the first time. It was easy and came so natural. I gave him my heart, in its entirety. I could love him unconditionally with my complete soul because opening my heart to him was without risk.

This was my very first experience with being in touch with my true nature, the natural state of love. This new ability to love proved to be very rewarding. This feeling multiplied when my second son was born, ten years later. By then, I was in a safer place in life, well on my path to spiritual awakening.

I fell truly, deeply, madly in love at first sight of my newborn baby and instantly love was redefined. In that same instant the new definition was etched into my soul. It felt like the missing piece to a puzzle I was unaware I was trying to solve. With insight and personal experience I could compare the high I experienced as the high people spend their lives trying to induce with chemicals. It was a pure love, the kind of love that feels like life energy feeding your existence. I could receive all the nourishment necessary for survival from love, removing the need for food or water. My son showed me that heaven wasn't somewhere we were hoping to get to. Heaven is right where you are standing; just follow the treasure map in your heart. I quickly became a love addict, as though I had tried heroin for the first time and was continually in search of another fix. I couldn't get enough. With this new-found addiction to the feeling of love, I began looking for it everywhere. I became acutely aware of love being the perfect replacement for a drug-altered state of mind.

Other peoples' love fed me as well. Watching a stranger as he gazes at his wife in adoration was something I finally understood. I got it. I knew what he was feeling. I had spent hours memorizing every detail of my sons face looking at him with those same adoring eyes. I once again believed in love and its power. Without realizing it, I was changing my frequency and tuning into my natural state.

The more I started to believe in love, the more I began to experience it everywhere. Love trickled into my life. I felt lighter, as if I could finally breathe. People and experiences that confirmed love existed started to show up in my reality every day. People were smiling at me. Old friends who still believed the love-is-a-myth mentality began to drift out of my life. I discovered love is everything. It is the power of the universe and the controlling element of all that is.

A new way of living had been shown to me, a way to translate everything. I had new lenses of love through which I could see the world. I started to find ways to love, not only for the man I share my bed with or the child that was born from my womb. I could love the man on the corner in need of a little assistance. I could love the guy who cut me off on the freeway. I could love my emotions even when they seemed irrational. I even began to love the air as I inhaled. I could love all of these things, and in return, I started to love and accept myself as whole and perfect just the way I was. My heart was wide open and opening more every day.

As I was tuning into a higher frequency, that frequency was being revealed everywhere. I discovered that the more I loved myself, the more I was able to see parts of me in every living thing I encountered. This love trickled into gratitude. When I felt love for people and things, I would then feel intense gratitude that those people and things had presented themselves in such a way that I was once again able to have my "love fix."

Love is like a catapult that can immediately launch you into a higher vibration. However, you do have to be careful to distinguish between love and lust, as they are very different and at opposite ends of the frequency scale. Lust is always directed at someone or something. It builds to a climax and dissolves away. However, you can feel love with or without an object of your affection. You can experience love in the stillness as you come into touch with your true nature. Love is life. It is the very fiber of our being.

"We perceive life through our lenses of experience."

A moment of revelation in my life bringing the clear and precise explanation of how we can be so confused about love, even mistaking abuse and pain as love, arrived when I heard this story during a foster parent training session:

baby Tina vs. baby Sue.

Tina's mom and dad had been dating for several years when he finally popped the question. Tina's mom was overjoyed as she said "yes." They worked hard and bought the house of their dreams. Shortly after the wedding ceremony, Tina's mom discovered that she was pregnant.

Tears of joy ran down her face as she hurried to the store to get everything that she would need in preparation for this beautiful angel to arrive.

Baby Sue's parents met at a party. Sue's mom had smoked some crack and woke up with Sue's dad on top of her. They continued to hang out, both helping one another to score more drugs. Sue's mom discovered she was pregnant only because she was arrested and the arresting officer noticed her protruding belly. Upon release, Sue's mom notified the possible father. Reluctantly, he accepted responsibility... sort of. Sue's mom never stops using drugs throughout her pregnancy and continues to have abusive, demeaning and unprotected sex with strangers.

When Tina was born, her mom and dad loved her with all of their hearts in a devotional, compassionate, selfless way. If she cried, they responded immediately to sooth her needs. As Tina's mom feeds and interacts with her, she gazes directly into Tina's eyes and talks in a soft, loving voice. Tina learns that when she experiences discomfort and cries, her parents respond with love and satisfy her needs. Tina grows to be a happy, well-adjusted two year old, meeting all of her growth milestones.

Sue was born addicted to meth and heroin. She spent the first few weeks of her life in a hospital, being tended to not by her cries but by the time on the clock. Sue's mom never comes to see her. When Sue goes home, her parents have no time or interest in her. Most of the time, they stick her in a playpen and close the door so they can't hear her cry. Her natural instinct to cry at discomfort is not met with an urge to sooth and console and instead is met with anger and frustration by her parents. Annoyed at the babies bothersome crying they yell at her and turn up the T.V. She never experiences eye contact or a loving gaze.

Nourishment is given through a bottle propped up by a blanket. At two years old, she barely walks unassisted and her vocabulary is minimal with a delay in her phonics. She avoids eye contact and shy's away from human contact. A neighbor finally calls child protective services, and CPS decides Sue's parents are unfit. Sue is removed from her home.

If Tina were to show up at your door as a foster child, she would be receptive to your open arms and your sweet melodic voice dripping with love and empathy. But to Sue, this would be a foreign language. She would have no understanding as to why you are trying to hold her and in her confusion may try to get as far away from you as she can kicking and screaming.

Love is a language we are taught. When this was explained to me, I was overwhelmed with a sense of understanding. How could I judge Sue for not adequately accepting my loving gestures? This began to free me from my judgment of others. It didn't mean that I necessarily accept what others do or always feel good about it, but, when I became able to see life through their eyes, I understood their veils and could let go of judgment.

"When you judge another, you do not define them. You define yourself."Wayne Dyer

When we stop judging others we can more clearly see ourselves. Even as I became old enough to travel to new places, the world around me didn't change. I could take a vacation to Hawaii and instead of seeing a tropical paradise I would see a seedy, drug ridden place filled with crime and violence. This was not my fault or a choice I was making, because other options are not available while you are still vibrating at such a low frequency. Being tuned into a low frequency, I could walk into a room filled with 999 saints and be drawn to sit next to the only sinner in the room...who, as I expected, would try to take advantage of me. Anyone tuned into a higher frequency would have experienced a room filled with love. That person would never even know that the single sinner existed.

When I searched my life for an example that best explains this concept, I remembered a walk I took with an old friend. I was now in my 30s and had significantly raised my vibration. I was choosing to have only experiences that involved seeing people in their highest state. My friend was still stuck in the old ways. Her life looked very different from mine. I saw beauty, love, smiles, and kindness everywhere I went. She had stories of sickness, disease, pain, theft, drugs, problems, and drama.

As our communication styles, and topics we enjoyed discussing changed, it produced a gap in our ability to connect in an enjoyable matter with one another. She wanted to share her views of people's situations in a negative way. I was starting to put a positive spin on the negative, viewing the good in everything. She didn't want to hear the good. I was recognizing that, in the past, people had judged and criticized me as well. Knowing the good intentions in my heart I wondered who was I to say that anybody else was any different. Everyone is somewhere on their path, even if this very moment is far from their final destination. We are all growing and in our growth we can use as much support as we can get. Participating in gossip or negativity wasn't an option for me anymore, and she no longer wanted to hear my optimism and happiness. Because of this, we had stopped speaking.

"You have power over your mind, not outside events. Realize this, and you will find strength." Marcus Aurelius, Meditations

My old friend and I had come together that day to take our dogs on a walk through this truly inspiring landscape that surrounded a small lake in our area. The walk was nice. I stayed positive and she played along. At one point towards the end of our walk, I noticed her attention was continually diverted to a group of people across a large field. I was enjoying the walk and almost completely unconscious of those people; my friend however, couldn't get them out of her mind. She started veering our path so we were now walking towards the group, who seemed to be searching for something in the grass.

Eventually we arrived at the site of the diversion, where my friend asked them what they were looking for. I wasn't sure why she had been so interested in them until I heard the answer: they were there as a result of a violent crime that had occurred at this site, where a teenager had been jumped and beaten. These kind people were searching for the teenager's wallet that he thought he might have dropped.

While this group was gathered to help, they were all thinking of and sending off fear around the crime that had happened. My friend, attuned to this same frequency, had been drawn toward it, while I had not. Saddened and feeling heavy, I was now finding it difficult to move my feet. I felt as though I had stepped into her frequency, where violent crimes and fear and hate were what ruled the world.
I would have never noticed, in the midst of all of the beauty, the one thing that could erase it all. She, however, tuned in immediately. Had we not been together on that walk we would have left with two incredibly different experiences.

I had shifted to a new frequency. I no longer felt

comfortable in old surroundings, around people I used to feel comfortable with. All it took was me wanting something more. I wanted to believe that life was more than what I had been living. I wanted the dream.

CHAPTER TWELVE

~Why We Stop Dreaming
and Start Settling~

When you were little, before the world got its hands on you, you trusted and had faith in those guiding you. You saw the world as a land of limitless possibilities. When I had played in this very street, right outside my home, wearing a tutu and carrying a wand, I believed in magic and thought that little people lived in the television. At the end of the rainbow there might be a pot of gold, protected by a leprechaun. Superman, Spiderman, and Wonder Woman were all very real, and maybe someday, my super powers would be revealed to the world, too. I had relied on my parents, as the key holders to the truth, to keep this magic alive.

Think back. There was a time when your imagination was fed and encouraged, when fairytales created your vision of the future. When you viewed the world through the eyes of your heart, before the veils and beliefs were established. The world looks very different when viewed from the heart, when the mind's purpose is to translate, not perceive. Our mind will tell us all the "why not's": there isn't enough, watch out, it will all fall to pieces. That is because society has planted these beliefs, and these beliefs now filter our reality. Our mind holds all of the information that either stops us or helps us expand into more of who we are. The mind stops us from stepping into the unknown, where all of the mysteries and miracles of life reside. The heart says, "Everything will work out perfectly; life is good. Trust, have faith and you can't fail." This is your truth, your natural state of being. You are capable of infinite creation, and are limited only by your beliefs.

Quiet your mind and trust in your heart and you will find the power of creation within you.

Remember when your parents, teachers, family loved it when you believed? They played along, leaving the cookies out for Santa. On Christmas morning, only one half-eaten cookie remained! Santa exists! He was here! Or your parents would wait until you fell asleep, then, snuck in your room to steal your tooth, leaving behind some money or pixie dust. They enjoyed watching you in your dreamy wonderland of infinite possibility.

"If you want your children to be intelligent, read them fairy tales. If you want them to be more intelligent, read them more fairy tales." Albert Einstein

The tradition continues to be passed on, until the coming of age brings forth the "It's time you should know" talk. This is the age that our parents have determined makes it time for us to "grow up."

Do you remember this time, when your parents told you that all of the fairytales are lies, tearing your foundation out from under you? Did they tell you that dreams and fairytales are silly, and you are different, not like us, if you still believe in them? Did they demand that you let go of the fantasyland and join "the real world," but then, in the same breath, tell you that the real world is dangerous and you can't trust anyone?

Our society has decided that this is the duty of a loving and protective parent: taking away all the good possibilities and replacing them with stress, worry, and fear. This is how we prepare our children as they embark into "the real world".

"I want to run through the halls in my high school. I want to scream at the top of my lungs. I just found out there is no such thing as the real world. Just a lie you have to rise above."
John Mayer

Your dreams and ideas of the world turn from a magical land of mystery to a fearful place of "dreams being diminished." At the age you enter into school, the ideas of a better world that, at one time, were embraced and encouraged are now dismissed and reflected back to you as a failure before you even try.

As children, we are driven intrinsically to create, to see a problem and fix it. Guided by your true nature, you will time and time again offer a solution, only to have all of the reasons it won't work thrust back at you. Eventually you might learn to stop offering solutions and, in hopes of being accepted and loved, start talking instead about the problem. When this happens, you have adopted a veil and are no longer able to see things through your true nature of hope, faith and possibility. Instead, you now see them through fear, failure and demise.

With everyone around you thinking and seeing things the same way, your beliefs are verified everywhere you look. When you tap into society's frequency, all forward movement is like running in place. Withdrawing from society and rebelling from mainstream thinking is the only solution to bring forth innovation and growth.

Your light was its brightest before you were able to truly understand mainstream concepts and ideas, before the brain developed its cognitive way of thinking. This is the early years from birth to toddler. Coincidentally, this is also a time where people are drawn to you like a magnet, because you hold the energy of enthusiasm about life. You live in a beautiful bubble of ignorance to the world's ways and, because of that ignorance, you live in bliss. Ignorance brings infinite possibilities: people can live on the moon and wishes on the stars do come true.

However, your ability to dream and have endless faith in your dreams cannot quite overpower Mom and Dad's beliefs and ability to limit your dreams. Eventually, when you tell your stories of space ships and aliens, they take in a deep sigh and, with great care, gently diminish your theories. In one fell swoop, they wipe away all the mysterious wonder. You are now one of them. They do not do this out of spite; rather, they are guided by love. They believe in their hearts they are doing this for your own good. You have contracted society's disease of limitation and locked yourself behind the imaginary boundaries of fear.

It only takes the dog one time being zapped as he crosses the imaginary fence line for him to know his boundaries and stay within them, even when not wearing the collar. This is what we do to our children: instill imaginary fences all around them, zapping them every time they step outside the line. A look of disapproval can be far more powerful than a sharp shock to the neck. The boundaries are set by those who love you. If they have spent their entire lives on the other side of those lines how can they feel safe letting you beyond them? You end up being taken only as far as the people you spend most of your time with have gone. Usually this is at least five steps back from where you started, where the world was your creation limited only by your imagination.

CHAPTER THIRTEEN

~Where Our Beliefs Come From~

The cure is found in surrendering to the deepest kind of faith:
that a power greater than you exists and it is good.

The day I returned to my childhood home, this is what I wanted: to remember that childlike sense of freedom that I once had. And when I did, I was able to clearly see all the beliefs I had accumulated that weighed me down. I had been making choices from a standpoint of which choice might lighten my burden, rather than with a sense of freedom to do or create anything that feeds my soul. Through the eyes of this new, childlike freedom, I asked myself, "Are these really MY beliefs? Do I know these beliefs are fact? Does it move me closer to my dreams to hold onto these beliefs?" The answer was an emphatic "NO!" It was then I lifted a veil that had been fogging my vision for a lifetime. Looking at that house and remembering the little girl I was, the joy of infinite possibilities came back to me.

Most adults are operating in a very limited reality, still carrying the beliefs of their parents and grandparents and then passing down these beliefs and disguising them as truths. It is all they know, and it is how they have created everything they have achieved. If you have worked every day of your life, barely getting by, and then telling a child that he or she can do what they enjoy and abundance will find them feels like a lie.

Examples of the beliefs running rampant these days are: *You have to work hard for your money*, interpreted by your soul as "go through the motions to provide for your family and put happiness and joy to the side," *you have to have money to make money,* or *money is the root of all evil.* These beliefs served a purpose at one time. These were the beliefs that kept you going from day to day. People go through their entire life believing that being a good person is achieved by going to work every day even if you are miserable and watching the clock praying for the hours to go by.

You are not serving society if you are unhappy. A peaceful society where everyone contributes starts with everyone finding their joy and connecting with their truth. Joy is derived from being of service *on purpose.* Only *you* know what that looks like. If you believe you are righteously sacrificing, and you see someone who isn't working living joyfully, with all of his needs met, you might feel discomfort and unease. You may experience anger because you see he has followed his dreams and lives on purpose, while you are sacrificing, even if you believe it is for the good of all. I can assure you that the person who is happy is making a much bigger contribution to our world than anyone who is doing what they feel they have to do and are bitter about it.

When the idea of sacrifice for the good of others was established as the way to be a good contributor in society, our world was very different. There wasn't the same technology that we have now. Inspiration to realization usually meant a lot of work and, most of the time, that work wasn't pleasant..

Our society has set expectations for our development, mentally and physically. One of these is when we are forced to change from the story that says *you can do anything you set your mind to,* to one that admonishes that *only a few special people are gifted with talent, and only they can shine above the rest.* When this happens, success is seen to come only through results of hard work and luck, and we measure our success by how much recognition, accolades, and acceptance the world gives us. In other words, we let society determine what success actually *is*. This is a direct path to pure misery, for there will always be people you cannot please no matter what you do. This has nothing to do with you and everything to do with them.

Some of the greatest people of our time— John Lennon, Mahatma Ghandi, and Martin Luther King, for example —were assassinated because someone didn't like their message of peace, love and oneness. But none of these men were working to please others. They were working from their heart on *behalf* of others. They were coming from a place of passion and purpose in service of the divine will. Their mission was selfless, and each of them left the world a better place because of their presence. They lived their truth and their truth lives on in us. The passing of their physical body has not stopped the influence of their essence that has permeated the planet.

You are here for greatness. The world needs you to live your truth. As you walk the path and tune into higher frequencies, you will draw more energy and vibrate at a higher level. The universe will begin to reveal itself to you. There will be others ahead of you on this path, lighting the way, and there with be others behind you, following the path by the light *you* shine. You must continue to grow and reveal the path to others as you discover it, just like John Lennon, Mahatma Gandhi, Martin Luther King, and so many others..

From What Beliefs do you Need to be Freed?

You have beliefs that are filtering your decisions, perceptions, and thoughts every day, beliefs that you have established about money, relationships, or love. Start to recognize your beliefs, and notice the way life verifies these beliefs *every day.*

Chapter Thirteen Worksheet:

Take a moment and revisit your childhood. Try and remember your first experience with money. Was it good or bad? Did you develop any feelings about money based on that experience? Go way back! Be honest! Here are some questions to help you.

Pull out our notebook and write down your answers:

THEN

- *When you were young, how was money presented in your home?*
- *As a child, did you view yourself as having a lot of money or was there never enough?*
- *What did the people around you say about money (your mom, dad, grandma, grandpa)?*
- *Try and remember your earliest memory of receiving or giving money. Write it down.*

NOW:

- *Do you see yourself currently as having enough, more than enough, or never enough?*
- *What do people you have around you now say about money? (i.e. friends complaining about bills or never enough to go anywhere or do anything)*

Revealing Your Beliefs

Take a look at your answers and see if you can find any beliefs that you have established about money. You might find that now, as an adult, you are continuing to prove to yourself the beliefs you established as a child. Remember that money is simply another energy that we work with in our lives: it either flows freely through us, allowing us to more easily influence the world, or it constricts us from moving freely in the direction of our dreams. It's likely that in your life, you have had to earn everything for yourself. Nothing was given to you. Because of this, you have a much greater appreciation for everything. You are able to be more empathetic to those that share in a lower money consciousness. You are caring, authentic, and wanting to contribute the most to the world.

However, if you are holding onto those old beliefs about money, you are hindering your own ability to create abundance in your life. You are literally blocking it from flowing freely to you. Perhaps there is an association of guilt and greed with expecting money to flow to you, which creates the opposite effect of what you most want. It constricts you, stopping you from maximizing your ability to contribute and influence the world for the better. You are spending too much time devoted to worry that there will not be enough.

Dare to dream in practical terms for financial abundance. Look at the sentence below and fill in the blank with whatever you feel passionate about. What ignites your spirit? Write this affirmation down and post it in as many places that you can and read it often.

It is my right to be abundant in all areas of my life, freeing me to…. (fill in the blank)!

Over the Rainbow

CHAPTER FOURTEEN

~The Midlife Crisis~

You have stayed in the lines, doing everything you were told.
Where is the joy and happiness you were promised?

Work is where mom and dad go every day and come home looking exhausted and complaining about all they had to do to provide the necessities for you. If you want to be loved and accepted by society, work isn't an option: it's an expectation. Society says, be responsible, not happy. It says that your value is based on your education or job title, and not on the level of joy you achieve. Your self-worth becomes something hung on a title that you carry, and people assume that your happiness level changes based on your job title.

This is absolute insanity! Happiness is not found in a title. Think about the sense of achievement and joy you may feel when you obtain a new label. Did it last for the rest of your life? My guess is, probably not. It is short-lived, because it is external.

Society may say that following your passion and joy is the sign of laziness, but nothing could be further from the truth. Following your passion and joy takes work, as it is ever fluctuating. In fact, you may appear to work *harder* than most people! The difference is that the satisfaction is found inward. You stop looking to society for affirmation that you can now be happy, because you no longer need the outside approval. When you live on purpose, the world can look you in the eye and call you an epic failure or tell you that you are a laughing stock, and all it does is put more steam in your engine. When others doubt you, root yourself deeper in faith.

When you live this way, you will come to a point where you will tip the scales and reach a faith level of 100%, unbreakable. This is pure magic. Your happiness will emanate from you with a luminous glow that needs no title, and people will experience it just by standing in your presence

We have all heard the term "midlife crisis." In our society, the path to happiness follows these stepping stone: Graduate high school. Go to college. Get a job, Buy a house. Get married, Start a family. Then, sit back and wait for the accolades, the pat on the back acknowledgement from the world which will finally bestow the sensation of happiness onto your life.

As a child, I watched my dad travel the "right path." At the end, his job gave him a watch and a dinner for his twenty-five years of service, his kids had left the house, and his marriage reflected his life: no passion, love, or zest. He had done everything right…yet he felt disappointed with the results, because he experienced life through the veil of "my happiness will arrive once I have done this."

"The pursuit of happiness is the source of all unhappiness. "
Lululemon

People all over the world who had done "all the right things," who have lived by the book, are wondering where their happiness is. The truth they didn't know is that happiness is found when you follow your passion and know your purpose. When you care deeply about what you are doing, life works. When you are happy, whole, and living on purpose, you want the rest of the world to share in your experience. Although following your purpose might not be socially acceptable at first, you will find that the more you fill yourself with your passion, the more the world will be drawn to you. You will become a selfless servant of mankind. You won't need anything from the world, because you will already feel fulfilled.

And here's the thing: when walking the path of your passion, there are no set steps for you to follow. Your path is unique to you and you only. It starts with a dream, *your* dream. What inspires you? What makes you want to get out of bed in the morning? When you have a dream, you will be guided and shown each step to effortlessly arrive.

> *It is the dream that gives you the journey,*
> *and the journey that gives you the joy*

You have to find happiness right where you are. It is never something that you are "working towards." Happiness is right here *in this moment, exactly as you are*. If you are "searching" for happiness, then you are telling yourself and the universe that you are not already experiencing happiness! This is an indicator that you are momentarily out of alignment with your passion and purpose. Don't place your happiness just out of reach. Don't say to yourself "Just one more thing and then I will be happy." The goal is to find happiness in this experience that you are currently having, with the things you already possess.

> *There is nowhere to go, except up*

Before I discovered this lesson, I lived life as if my joy were just out of reach. There were always things I needed to take care of in order to finally experience joy. I hadn't yet realized that it was because I had adopted the state of mind that I would *always* have things I must do before I could find joy, that I was continually struggling. I was very stubborn in this belief, and so the universe was very crafty: it took everything away and dropped me to the very bottom, where I had nothing left to lose. There, I discovered that I could find joy in every little thing because I was no longer in fear of losing anything!

We are all presented with transitional moments throughout our lives. Usually you find yourself at an intersection with two paths going in opposite directions. Each of us has a special journey; you are on the path that is only yours. Each step along the way is a series of lessons.
I used to view it as a ladder we climb to the heavens, each wrung a new lesson. Permission to ascend is granted when the lesson is learned. Often is seems that you spend more time falling off the ladder completely, than making any progress on your journey to the desired destination. One thing I have learned is; it is always easier to choose which way to go when there is only one option; up! This is why hitting rock bottom, as I did, is often a sign you have finally stumbled upon the right path!.

Even though you are on the right path, the climb back up is steep and treacherous. The terrain isn't easy and it is hard to find stable footing. Every mountain climber starts out slow and easy with a few falls before they make it to the top. It takes practice to get good at ascending the side of a mountain. But, the first mountain conquered is invigorating and at the top, a whole new world reveals itself on the other side. With most of my life being a slow steady decline this was new for me. The fall to the bottom left me a fragmented version of myself, and it was hard to see my destination while I was holding broken pieces together.
Each time you slip back down you are getting stronger, more confident and within that strength and experience is a lesson. It is hard reliving a lesson you thought you had mastered. Once you recognize why you have fallen again,

you can fly past all the steps with ease, back to the top.

I had fallen so many times, I wasn't even sure which way was up. Until I found myself in that 8X8 holding cell, surrounded by people I never wanted to be like. I knew this was the real bottom. In this tiny room sat ten or more women, with hollow eyes, sunken-cheeks, faces filled with scabs. Some rambled to themselves in the corner. I watched as a woman got up and walked over to the toilet in the center of the room, squatted with her pants around her ankles and pulled something out of her vagina. Each one of them in their own world as if no one else existed. The women at the toilet pulled out some tin foil and in no time carefully crafted a crack pipe.

I was stewing in my anger. My freedom wasn't something I appreciated until the very moment it was taken. Held captive by my jailers and forced to sit in the vicinity of crack being smoked. Yes, I did drugs. But, in my mind I would never sink so low as to smoke crack! I differentiated myself from the crack smoker like our society distinguishes us with classes. I was a much higher class drug user, so I thought. Why would they put me in here? Couldn't they see how different I was from these people? I was a mother, a daughter, a friend, not a criminal in need of incarceration! I was *me*!

That was when I realized the answer was, "No." They couldn't see that I was different, *because I wasn't*. My radio frequency was on the same channel as all those people I was sharing that cell with. That moment was a victory in my life because it opened my eyes. With a new appreciation for freedom I was ready to change my frequency and thankfully, there was absolutely nowhere to go but up.

Over the Rainbow

CHAPTER FIFTEEN

~Find Contentment Where You Are~

*"All men should strive
to learn before they die
what they are running from, and to, and why."*
~ James Thurber

Someone had tried to stop me from running once. He had said to me, "no matter where you run, you will always be there. Contentment is found within. You can't keep running, eventually you will have to stop and look within." At the time I wasn't ready to receive this lesson but now I see what he meant with crystal clarity.

By the time I paid back the Karma bank a healthy dividend of $13,000, I had been traveling and experiencing a little more of what the world had to offer. I had noticed that no matter where I went, I was unable to find contentment. I wanted peace of mind. I felt as though I hadn't stopped running from the day I left home. I had burned bridges everywhere and never cared because the moment I started to care an overwhelming feeling that was foreign would send me into the arms of any substance that could create a momentary separation from reality. If things got too uncomfortable I would move my physical body to a new place…and in the new place discover that I was not able to escape the invisible chains around my ankle.

As hard as I tried, I couldn't seem to outrun *me*.

In the bible, Jesus is asked "Where is the kingdom of God?" He responds "The kingdom of God is within you." My interpretation of what god was saying that has guided me in my life is, there is no need to travel anywhere to find what is right there, already inside you. The entire kingdom of God is at your fingertips all the time. All you have to do is get quiet and go within to experience it.

As you set off on your path, remember that as you cleanse your body of the toxins you have been feeding it—drugs, alcohol, and fast foods—you will be forced to face the feelings and situations that you started those habits to hide from. Whatever is dwelling deep in your subconscious that you have not done the work to shine the light of awareness on becomes like venomous snakes, ready to strike at any time as your weakness reveals itself. When this happens, resist the urge to turn back to whatever "anti-venom" you have relied on in the past for a cure from the pain.

A clean mind has a clear view. Buddhist teachings stress the importance of mindfulness as part of the path to self-awareness or enlightenment. To be mindful, you must have a constant awareness of changes occurring in the mind and body. Mindfulness enables you to react wisely to emotions and sensations when they arrive. Alcohol and drugs distort the mind's ability to do this.

Karma is something else that is very important to the teachings of the Buddha. These teachings were present in my life before I had officially studied Buddhism and now, many years later; I have seen the parallel as I have sat at the feet of many masters and spent many hours in contemplative thought after meditation. All the teachings speak to the fact that you must be responsible for your own karma. Only you are responsible for your own actions, thoughts, and words. You will discover the door to all happiness is in choosing the right thoughts. It is like finding the password to open the door. "Open sesame." Some thoughts open doors while others you can perceive to close doors.

Heaven is right here on earth, and the gates to heaven are through your heart. The path is found in the stillness.

Meditation is taught in most eastern religions, and ancient texts report it as a way to purify the mind, cultivating presence by connecting with stillness. In the stillness the waters of the mind become clear and thoughts intent on guiding you towards happiness can penetrate deep into your subconscious where they will serve the highest power.

On several occasions, I have had the opportunity to sit with a Zen Buddhist master. Each time I took away something new, something that he had heard or experienced in the silence of meditation. One beautiful metaphor that really spoke to me was seeing your minds as a snow globe, those little versions of cities or miniature scenes within a bubble-shaped glass, filled with water and white flakes settled at the bottom. When you shake the snow globe, the water becomes cloudy as the flakes move around to resemble snow falling. This cloudiness is just like our minds. Throughout the day our minds become clouded with thoughts floating around, making it hard for us to see clearly. Meditation is the act of stillness and quieting the mind. All of the snow settles at the bottom of the glass and the water becomes clear again, so we can see.

When the mind is pure and you have found an inner peace, you will have no need to run. You can travel the world in search of happiness but only find it once you arrive back to yourself. The deepest truths cannot be understood through spoken word. They are discovered in the silence. Although I had been told these truths I had to see them for myself. I traveled the world in search of peace and came up empty-handed...until the day I discovered yoga. Yoga is what took me home and I embarked on a whole new world exploring the depths of the self.

Yoga is the yoking of the mind, the body, and the spirit. This connection means you stop fighting what is and start accepting it. This is where the liberation of all suffering lies.

Yoga was my answer. It was my ability to look within and sort through all of the clutter. I learned how to deal with my pain and love myself in spite of my experiences. I learned to forgive myself for allowing that younger me to be wounded. I was finally able to find my peace of mind. When I started practicing yoga in my early 20s, it was as if a light switch went off inside of me illuminating a whole other world within me that I hadn't yet seen.

Yoga was able to retune my frequency to rise above society. Through my practice, I would make a connection with the divine and feel a frequency that transcended all others. This was better than any drug I could take. The frequency was one of healing old wounds and scars on both my physical body and my psyche. The high was indescribable, heaven expressed on earth in the confines of my own mind. This higher frequency allowed the world to change right before my eyes. I saw goodness where I hadn't before and felt peace where I never had.

Finding your Sedona

We have forgotten that we have magical powers. Somewhere along the way we have misplaced our magic wands. Yoga is a tool designed specifically for recalibrating your antennae to the divine. The practice demands a quiet mind in stillness the elements of sounds created by uttering

Sanskrit words and breathe unleashes the flow of vital life force energy throughout the body. This energy is vibrating at the frequency of life, healing, truth, balance and well-being. By the end of the class everyone has tuned in and all of their bodies are vibrating at this frequency which is directly linked to the divine. That link is your magic wand.

There are places in the world where those who are sensitive and aware of energy can experience a shift, that could be construed as an open line of communication with the divine much like the one created through yoga postures, meditation and breathing.

Sedona, Arizona has a reputation as a spiritual Mecca, filled with global power spots or vortex sites. A vortex is a site where the energy of an area is concentrated at its center. As a deliberate creator of your life, you will find you are more sensitive to energy. When you are in a vortex site, this represents a pocket of heightened consciousness and creation. You are more easily able to connect with and reveal source as the unfoldment of your life. A vortex or power site is conducive to prayer, healing, and meditation, recalibrating your frequency and realigning your connection to the divine. Native Americans have used these vortexes as places to perform their devotional ceremonies for ages.

As awareness spreads through our planet, so does the number of healers, light workers, intuitives, artists, and spiritual guides that are drawn to these vortex sites. Looking to get recharged by plugging directly into a source of divine energy. In my studies, I have drawn the conclusion that pockets of high consciousness are everywhere, and that they are easily recognizable, maybe by a beautiful, lush landscape, by seemingly indestructible buildings that hold the mystery of their creation, or by the way they take the imagination on a journey to the unthinkable. Imagine the pyramids in Egypt or Stonehenge, or any of the Seven

Wonders of the World. It took highly-tuned consciousness to create these wonders and still nobody has a viable explanation.

The easiest way to spot vortex sites is by the ability of the site to flourish with ease. Think of the oasis in the middle of the desert. Scarcity, struggle and very few life forms exist in the heat of the desert sun. Then, in the midst of nothingness a flourishing metropolis appears. Suddenly there is life! You have found a vortex site. It is important to learn to recognize these pockets of high consciousness, not just for divine reconciliation with the universe or creation, but also for yourself: because these are the places you want to build a business or a home if you want to be successful. While honing your awareness rely on others who have already tuned in. Learning to connect with higher frequencies or energy can begin with observing the habits of people who seem to have what you want. Where do they go to recharge? Simply follow their lead.

We all need to have a sacred place, a place where we can go to feel more connected to our source, higher power, deity or god. After my discovery of yoga, I tuned into the places that held a higher energy or vibration for me, allowing me to stay in the higher frequencies. I found that anywhere close to a body of water is that place. It is my monastery, synagogue, church, and temple, the place I turn to feel better. Just sitting at the edge of the water seems to mend all of my cracks. There are times I have felt as though I was one small breeze away from crumbling into pieces, never to be put back together again, only to be healed immediately as I sat at the water's edge. The water connects me to that place where I let go of trying to make it perfect and begin to see that it already *is* perfect.

It is important to know what feeds your soul. As you

are reintroduced to your true self as a spiritual being you will once again know what it feels like when your soul is flourishing, and you will search for ways to nourish it. Ask yourself "where am I when I am most inspired." Sit with Mother Nature and all her magnificent beauty. Find this place in your home or areas near your home and visit it as often as you can.

~*The big me revisiting the small me*~

It took twelve years to emancipate myself from the manifestation of my limiting beliefs revealing itself in the unfoldment of my life. For twelve years I sold my body, mind and spirit in various ways. This was the foundation from which my entire life was being built. Now, many years had passed and my path had led me here, sitting in my old neighborhood. I was there hoping to fill in the missing pieces and find answers. I had emerged out of Dante's inferno, lingered in purgatory, and was finally seeing glimpses of heaven. Why me? Why are so many souls still trapped in my old life? Unable to emerge out of the depths within their endless cavern of hurt, pain and an overall sense of worthlessness, while I escaped and discovered a whole new world that seemed to materialize right before my eyes. These questions sent me on a quest for the truth.

I looked with amazement at the place that had, at one time, locked me outside the gates of heaven. Having been the source of all of those thoughts clouding my mind and closing doors, it felt surprisingly far away, as though many lifetimes had passed since I was that little girl. The street in front of my childhood home was filled with those lifetimes. I could hear the laughter and see us playing make believe. There, on my front lawn I had once stood, wearing my ballet recital outfit, filled with dreams of happily ever after.

For just a moment, one very pivotal moment, I felt the sensation of true freedom, a feeling that can only be described as heaven. The key had been there all along! It was just hidden behind all the layers that society had placed over my true self. When I washed away all of the layers that life had placed on me and returned to my truest nature, I discovered that life had been there, waiting for me to open my eyes and see. I woke up.

I had found what I was looking for. Even if it was only a glimpse, it was powerful. I felt engulfed by the kind of freedom that has no restrictions or boundaries. I had once again returned to the land where anything is possible.

Today as I move through my life, that sensation comes and goes. I use it as my compass. If I believe in myself and my ability to create and all doubt is gone, I am on the right path to living my life on purpose. If I feel as though life is difficult and I don't have enough time, money, energy, help etc. to fulfill my dreams, then I know that I need to recalibrate my compass by finding that feeling I felt on that truly extraordinary day outside my childhood home.

Section Two

How to find your Passion and Purpose

What do you really want?

What exactly is the Law of Attraction?

How do you apply These concepts to your life?

Over the Rainbow

CHAPTER SIXTEEN

~*The Power of Light*~
~*Allow the light to come in and transform the darkness* ~

After discovering my contentment and deepening my connection to the higher frequency, I began on a path to mastering what I had learned. In my mid 20s I had been doing a lot of research around the concept referred to as, "Law of Attraction". I began to see parallel's, recognizing similarities in concepts such as Newton's law, which states; that every *action has an equal and opposite reaction*, karmic law (what you give out you get back), and the overall understanding that justice, truth, and intent all state that I am responsible for my own reality. My actions, thoughts, and words all add color to the canvas that is my life. Everything that has happened in my life until this point I have created, and I continue to add to the masterpiece with every breath I take. Living with an understanding of The Law of Attraction, I began to understand that I was never a victim of bad luck or circumstance. I studied and read old and new scripture. I took seminars and went to temples and monasteries, absorbing as much information as I could. I came to the conclusion that there is no such thing as a predetermined destiny or fate. There is always only what you believe and the choice between fear or faith in any given moment.

Accepting this idea meant that I must accept that I created everything in my life. I didn't get to pick and choose. Of course, some of this was easy to believe. I chose to be a good mom and raise my son with a caring, secure home. I chose to get away from the painful places I had been and rely on my strength and perseverance to survive and provide for myself and my son.

It took a little longer to own the idea that not only did I get myself out of those situations but that I had placed myself in those situations as well. Through my thoughts and actions—whether or not I was aware of it or unconsciously creating it—I had created those painful, scary places filled with abuse and emptiness. I needed those experiences in order to become who I was intended to become. I needed the opportunity to build strength and character and to be able to empathize with others who are finding themselves in the vicious circle of lack and scarcity. I had to look to the experiences for the lessons.

Simply stated, The Law of Attraction, starts with asking yourself, "Can I believe that bad luck and circumstance doesn't exist? Can I accept that there are no such things as success and failure? Can I really accept that everything in my life, with no exceptions, I have created?" Accepting every part of my life as perfect allowed me to answer those question with a "yes" and believe it, while feeling grateful, without bias, for *every* event that I had experienced in my life. Believing that to be true meant I couldn't cry out "Why me?" in the middle of the night anymore. How could I feel sorry for myself and at the same time take ownership as a true creator? Who was I calling out to when the only person with that answer was me? I could no longer blame an unfortunate series of events for the hardships that were being presented in my life. It became clear that everything that was happening was a mirror, reflecting what was inside of me. Sometimes I was being presented with lessons or revealing weakness, sometimes I was being shown what I *didn't* want as life's way of allowing me to become clearer about what I *did* want.

Reprogramming myself brought more difficulty and discomfort than I had anticipated. I realized that I was going to have to really work at this new way of approaching life. So, I set out in search of a school to hone these techniques. Life became that school. It was miraculous how pieces would fall together and how often I would find myself smiling in amazement as life brought little synchronicities and my thoughts materialized as things. I spent a few years in this field of study until I was ready to start sharing what I had learned.

In my late 20s I facilitated a group where others interested in these concepts gathered in support of one another. At this point in my life, I had been gifted with many great teachers. I had gone to seminar after seminar on The Law of Attraction principles. I had read hundreds of books. I had practice yoga, meditated, and studied spiritual texts with master teachers and guides
Some of the participants were already familiar with the principles of The Law of Attraction, while some were just curious and not sure what exactly had drawn them there. The goal of the group was to help transform consciousness and use The Law of Attraction techniques to take ownership of our lives and create the life of our dreams. It was a venue for me to share the powerful truths I had discovered on my path while giving me an environment to learn and absorb more through the collective consciousness of a group.

The power of light in the midst of darkness

At the time, the economy was changing. Fear was everywhere, as all of those weak foundations built by society's need to find validation in material goods started to crumble and fall. People were losing their homes to foreclosure, cars were being repossessed, the unemployment rate was increasing, and businesses were closing down. Relationships were falling apart due to these financial burdens. The added stress was causing people's health to decline. The few people who stayed afloat were the ones that never lost faith, the ones who avoided the naysayers and didn't watch the news or read the newspaper. They created their own beliefs and chose to not be influenced by what the world was telling them was true. This population is always small, but able to make a huge impact! They propel change and forward movement.

Transformation was within our grasp. Many people turned to faith as they had nowhere to go but up. People were able to peer through what the media sells as important and return to seeing what really mattered. As all of their material possessions were being carted away, they looked around at what was left and discovered those were the only things that really matter: your family, your friends, your faith. People had started forming their identity by what they had or what they did; now they had to love themselves for who they were, as all of those things were stripped away, leaving behind a new sense of vulnerability and truth.

Everything you once dreamed of is waiting for you to make it part of your reality

What you see around you is what you have created. Yes, you built the castle made of sand. You tricked yourself into believing it was bricks and mortar until the light shined upon it and dried out all of the water causing the sand to fall to the ground. Now, as you look around, what you see is what you believe. Some of us have chosen to believe that we are in a terrible recession and we must start to prepare for the fall of society as we know it. Others have decided this is the perfect time to build their empire and help to forge a new society built on foundations of peace, love, happiness, joy and the entire population free of fear, living the life of their dreams.

The good news is, you are the dreamers, those few that the world is counting on to redesign and recreate a world based on the beauty that already exists. You have always seen beauty that other people weren't able to see. The world has always revealed its perfection to you, and you probably wondered why others couldn't see what you saw. When you believe in yourself, others will believe in you, too.

Over the Rainbow

CHAPTER SEVENTEEN
~*It All Began as a Thought*~
The Law of attraction

"All that we are is a result of what we have thought. If a man speaks or acts with an evil thought, pain follows him. If a man speaks or acts with a pure thought, happiness follows him, like a shadow that will never leave." Buddha

Your beliefs and expectations create everything that you see in every moment. It is an illusion. Your mind is the gifted artist responsible for the painting that is your life. Close your eyes and see if you can create a new vision. Take out your brush, invoke the spirit of your muse and see your life as an empty canvas waiting for divine inspiration. Think of what colors you wish to use and design your landscape. Imagine special paint brushes each with the ability to apply to your canvas, one of the five senses. If you would like to create more abundance in your life, allow the stroke of the scent brush to bring the smell of money, or the scent of ink as it goes onto a check being written to you. What sounds would the pen make as it moves across the paper? Allow the brush of sound to apply it to the canvas. The stroke of the feeling brush brings the feeling of the check or money in your hands and the sensation joy or relief into your body. Painting what you see, hear, feel, smell and even taste onto the canvas of your life is the mastery of manifestation or the essence of the Law of Attraction. Get so detailed that you could describe it to someone else and they would be able to see your masterpiece in their mind, too.

Pull out your notebook. Open to the next blank page and write at the top "*I wish..*" Then write all of your wishes as clearly as you can see them displayed on your canvas. See them in your mind's eye as your describe them on paper.

Then turn to the next page and write at the top "*I have...*" On this page rewrite each of your wishes as if you already have them. Write with words of gratitude and feelings of joy. i.e. I am so grateful that I have such a wonderful, loving relationship filled with passion. I love living in my new house and gazing at the beautiful garden. Do this as if you are already living your dreams and you are so filled with gratitude. On the third page write at the top "*I deserve...*" Fill this page with all the reasons you deserve these dreams to be a part of your life. Keep this journal with you and read it often!

What is the Law of Attraction?

The Law of Attraction is like beautiful poetry. It creates a spectacular vision that emanates from the depths of your innermost being out into the universe and is reflected back to you in everything, everywhere. Living this law takes mastery of two simple concepts. The first concept is: *like attracts like*. As in the saying "birds of a feather flock together," we draw to us—and find ourselves drawn to—people or things that demonstrate the same habits, hobbies, pastimes, and beliefs that we do. This is true for positive, life-affirming experiences as well as for negative ones. The people that you surround yourself with are a good indication of where you are in your life. The qualities that you recognize in them are the qualities you brought them into your life to reflect back to you about yourself. You will draw to you people with similar beliefs, thoughts, and experiences.

For example: If you love sports, you will tend to bring experiences of watching, reading about, or playing sports into your life. In doing those things, you will find yourself around other people that share that interest. You will notice ads or articles in magazines or on TV that refer to sports.

Billboards or people that are wearing clothing that might indicate they, too, enjoy sports may stand out. On the other hand, someone else who has never played, watched, or had the tiniest interest in sports, would not have noticed or paid attention to any of these things.

Try and remember the last time that you bought a car. Before you purchased your car, you had never noticed a white Nissan Altima on the road. When you bought your new white Nissan Altima, suddenly they seemed to be everywhere you looked! Did the Nissan dealership happen to sell hundreds of these cars at the same time you bought yours, or is your awareness just tuned in white Nissan Altimas?

Imagine the first time you tried sushi or Thai food. You may have noticed an occasional sushi place in your area before and not paid much attention to it. Then your friend finally persuades you to try something new, before you know it you are at their favorite sushi house. Closing your eyes, being adventurous, and showing your friend that you are open to new things, you finally place that first bite of a sushi roll past your lips and, to your surprise, its love at first taste. The next day, as you drive around the same town you have lived in for eight years, you begin to notice sushi places everywhere, as if they were all built overnight. They had always been there, but you weren't looking for them.

We only see what we believe is possible. We match patterns that already exist within us through conditioning. A story that demonstrates this perfectly is the story of when Columbus first came to the new world. As the ships were first arriving to the new world, it is said that the native shaman came to the edge of the water. This shaman had no way of knowing that Columbus and his ships were approaching; he was just following his inner guidance as he approached the edge of the water and stood looking off into the horizon.

He could see the water moving in a strange way. The ripples were telling him that something was moving the water. However, his conscious mind could not see the ships, because he was incapable of seeing something so far outside of his realm of perception. Although large ships barreled down on him, clearly visible, they were not able to register on his consciousness, making them visible to the human eye.

The shamans were relied upon as the seers, people with strong intuition who and could see things that others could not. They were the healers and protectors who could sense danger in advance, giving their people a chance to escape to safety. According to this story, this shaman stood there, staring at the ripples in the water, until finally he was able to see the ships materialize. Then he was able to describe these ships to everyone else. Believing so deeply in the shaman, the power of belief allowed them to finally see the ships too. How much is going on right now, directly in front of our eyes, without us being able to see it?

When I inhabited the world of low vibration, tuned into a low frequency, I was incapable of seeing the good that was right there. I could not see the boats coming into shore; I saw only water rippling. It wasn't until I started to retune myself that I could see all that had been hidden in the shadows. At first they were blurry, but with enough focus and intention, I could finally see my freedom in high definition. If you can believe in these words as those people believed in their Shaman good can appear just as quickly for you as the boats did for them.

The human brain receives billions of bits of

information every day. We process only a very small amount of this information. We filter out information that is unimportant to our daily routines. We also have a tendency to slightly warp the information that we do receive so it better fits our attitudes and perspectives. Each of us holds our own perception of what happens. Five people could all attend the same event and walk away with five completely different stories. This would be even more powerfully displayed if all five people came from drastically different backgrounds, cultures, and walks of life.

How our brains recognize patterns depends on our familiarity with what we are seeing. I remember reading about the astounding experimental work of Cambridge researchers, Colin Blakemore and G.F. Cooper, proving the ability to see isn't born in us, but must be learned. Blakemore and Cooper reared kittens in darkness for five hours a day when the kittens were placed in environments rigged so they could see only black and white, horizontal or vertical stripes. They wore cones to hinder them from seeing their own bodies. When later exposed to a dangling black rod, the felines reared with horizontal stripes could see the rod only when it was positioned horizontally. As the rod was turned vertically, only the vertical world kittens saw it. The rod "disappeared" in the eyes of the horizontal world kittens. Deprived of experience with the other plane, each group of kittens was incapable of seeing it. Their visual cortices didn't develop the cells to see the horizontals or verticals they'd never experienced. What is there, right in front of us, that we can see?

The first time I saw one of those holographic 5D pictures, I was unable to see the artistic integrity. All I could see were a bunch of jumbled-up colors and symbols that meant nothing. The picture was titled, "The Great Eagle." Figuring that there must be something more to see, I followed the instructions on the back, which said: *Let the eyes move out of focus, allowing them to go blurry. They may begin to water or sting. Let the subconscious mind reveal the picture.*

Although I was eventually able to allow the picture to reveal itself, it was not an easy task. I am also quite certain that had I not known what I was looking for I may have never seen it, no matter how long I stared. It was amazing how the eagle materialized and popped right out of the picture. Each time I looked at that picture, it became easier and easier to see, until one day I was looking at the picture and that is all I saw.

~Where attention goes,
Energy flows~

The second concept in the law of attraction is*: Where attention goes, energy flows.* This is demonstrated in the examples above, however it goes a step further. If everything already exists and is just waiting patiently for you to reveal it, then it makes sense that abundance is everywhere, just waiting for you to see it and take some. The problem is, "where attention goes, energy flows." You have to look at where you are placing your attention. Just like the Shaman had to look at the water with the intent of seeing it before it could materialize, you must look to something that you can't yet see with faith that it is there.

If you are experiencing a lack of something, you are usually focused on the *not having.* You are *expecting* to reveal lack! This is where your attention is. Prosperity is all around you and just like the kittens in the tubes you have been programmed to see lack. You are blind to the prosperity. I Know it is difficult to turn your attention in the direction of already having something that all of your senses are saying isn't there. *Focus or attention is the creator.* Nothing can exist until we look at it and agree that it is there. This is something that goes against our very nature, all the way down to the core of our being. We are shown our whole lives that we have to look to the problem and analyze it to find the solution. This is simply not true. Looking at the problem and analyzing it will only draw more of the problem to you. You will start to see evidence everywhere proving that you don't have enough money or that nobody loves you. The only reason that lack of anything ever shows up in your life is because you turned your attention in the direction of lack.

The only way to solve a problem is to decide what the solution will look, and feel like. Neville Goddard says it best when he says: *"The future dream must become a present fact in your mind. You must experience in imagination what you would experience in reality in the event you achieved your goal, for the soul imagining itself into a situation takes on the results of that imaginary act. So the key is to disregard all the evidence of your five senses. What you see, hear, feel, smell, and experience in your reality is not your truth. Your truth is what you imagine and dream your life to be. When you can do this, it will be."* Get out your paint brushes and start to paint your new reality.

"For I have saw it- let no man see through my vision-It is as I choose - as I want —as I can let it be so" Neville

An example of The Law of Attraction at work: The power of light was helping me as the teacher to grow as the student as well. I was testing these theories and getting more in touch with who I was and what I wanted to contribute. I was teaching people to follow their passions and let that be their gift to the world, and I was discovering that real estate, as a career, was no longer serving that purpose for me. I saw that more of my time was spent practicing yoga and sharing my discoveries on the yogic path with anyone who would listen.

I knew it was time to start pursuing my dreams to live and breathe yoga all day, every day, as well as to guide others on their spiritual journeys. I just didn't know how. At the time of this decision, real estate was falling to pieces. I was a single mom, with two kids now. I had a mortgage I wasn't able to pay, leaving my house pending foreclosure. I focused on revealing the good. I knew that everything was happening exactly as it should be and my life was unfolding perfectly on track to reveal my highest good. However, my faith was being tested. Even at the very lowest point, could I still believe it was going to all work out in favor of my highest good?

At this point I knew that my heart was yearning to own a yoga studio and help to bring love to the community on a greater scale. With my world crumbling around me, and with the fact that I had no official yoga teacher training or teaching experience, it seemed like an impossible dream. The only way to explain my conviction is this: I had a knowing greater than anything my artificial; ego-self was capable of take over my heart. It told me that it will be. I, in trust and in faith, said, "if you promise it will be, then I will take the steps you show me." From that day on I was divinely guided.

The first step was the hardest to see because the path wasn't yet clear. This is always true. So you must be open and aware at all times with your heart, vision, and focus always on the dream. On my way home one day, I got a call from one of the members of my group, "Power of Light." They asked me what I was doing today to move in the direction of my dream. This was a question I often asked them, and I was a little uneasy hearing the question coming back to me. My response was, "There is nothing I can do today! I don't have the money for the training necessary to teach and I can't teach until I have the training!" He responded again, reflecting myself and my words back to me "How do you know that for sure? Have you tried teaching? There must be some way you could get experience. Why not hold a class in your home?" I was blind to my own blocks. It was so easy to see them in everyone else and diminish their validity, but, I could hear and feel the conviction in my voice and body to hold onto my blocks as real and valid.

This block was my opportunity to be a student as well as the teacher. How could I continue telling others that they must move past *their* blocks if I let mine stop me? It is so easy to see and point out imagined boulders of old beliefs, when you are standing on the outside. When you are the one with the boulder sitting right in the middle of your path, you often can't see around it. So you lose sight of the dream just on the other side. Gaining clarity and climbing over them or shattering them into tiny pieces just by denying their truth reveals your dreams once again. And now they look attainable.

It turned out that shattering the boulder to pieces didn't take a giant rocket launcher. In fact, very little artillery was needed to crush that block. Still on the phone with me friend, I looked to my left and saw I was passing a small, family-owned gym. I had passed it hundreds of times as it was less than five miles from my house. Looking at the gym, I thought to myself that I would prove my friend wrong and go in the gym and ask about a job. I walked into the gym prepared for rejection. Standing behind the counter chewing gum, talking on the phone, and showing absolutely no interest in me as I stood quietly waiting for my opportunity to dazzle her, was a young, beautiful ponytail-having, spandex wearing girl. Realizing I wasn't going anywhere, she finally glanced up and, with a sigh that reeked of slightly annoyed, asked the person on the other end of the phone if she could call them back. Placing the phone on the receiver, she looks at me and says, "Can I help you?"

I respond with an "Ummm... Yes." At this point I just wanted to leave, but I finally mustered the courage to ask if they were looking for any yoga teachers.

"Are you certified?" she asked

"No." I responded expecting that would be the end of the conversation. But it got worse.

"Do you have your CPR training?"

Again I answered, "No."

The next question came: "Do you have your blood pathogens cert?"

By now I was feeling even worse "No."

To my surprise, her next response was, "Well, I guess we could use you to fill in from time to time. When are you available?"

I almost fell over. Without delay, I said, "Now." She told me that they wouldn't be able to pay me much since I wasn't certified.
I said "No problem!"

"Work alone is your privilege, never the fruits thereof. Never let the fruits of action be your motive; and never cease to work...Be not affected by success or failure. This equipoise is called Yoga."
~as quoted in Light on Yoga

I would have been willing to teach for free. It felt as if I was living in a dream. Being willing to work for free is a sure sign that you are working on purpose, filled with passion. If you are willing to do it for free, with excellence and devotion, even if the world tells you are crazy, then you have discovered a step in the direction of your contribution to this world. And know that you have a special contribution that is all yours to give. You are a gift that the world has been waiting to open!

I started right away. Before long I was teaching all of the classes and they were full! Everyone raved about my style and I was getting invaluable, hands-on experience. Without my asking, the gym tripled my pay. I was on my way to having my own studio. I was beginning to see the path.

Still experiencing a financial hardship but holding onto faith, life had brought me to my knees once again. On my knees I clasped my hands together and surrendered. I looked up as though I was at the bottom having released all attachments. I had no more fears because releasing my attachments I had nothing left to lose. This was actually freeing. Asking the question "What is the worst that can happen?" from a place of experiencing what at one time would have been your answer to that question, losing your home, your business and all of your security, brings a feeling of invincibility.

"I am invincible… as long as I'm alive." John Mayer

It started like any other day. But, on this day something snapped. I was in my car driving down a very familiar street when I noticed I was on autopilot. I instantly dove back into my body and from the center of my being yelled "Wake up!!" In this awakening I looked out of my eyes and explored my surroundings. I looked at my hands on the steering wheel as though I was seeing them for the first time. I looked at my dash and out my windshield and imagined I was in a dream. If I was in my dream I thought, then I have a choice. "Is this what I would choose?" I pulled the car over and really looked around. And, a scream came from within "NO!" I wish to own a yoga studio. I asked that voice from within "What is my first step?"

I had been working with an investor that was taking advantage of the condition of the economy and buying commercial properties that were being foreclosed on by the bank. I picked up my phone and still sitting on the side of the road I called him and said "I want a yoga studio." His response came without hesitation. "Okay, where?" I mentioned the area I was interested in and he immediately gave me an address of a property he had been looking at. The steps began lining up in front of my and all I had to do from there was step on them.

The next night I was teaching a class at the gym and casually mentioned "When I have my own studio the space would be sacred and we could honor the true traditions of yoga." After class, one of my students approached me and said, "Did you mean what you said when you said you wanted your own studio?" I replied, "Yes." Her response floored me, "I want to give it to you. My husband and I are inheriting some money due to the passing of his mother and we have been looking for an investment. Would you be interested in working with us?" What was once a dream became a reality.

The Studio would not be the end of my growth but, the beginning. Soon after opening, my faith was again tested. I had firsthand experienced my ability to create something from nothing. I was witness to the limitless power of the universe. I was a believer, in the truest form, in the Law of Attraction. I could not see the possibility of failure. However, I was still fighting off society's sickness and my immune system would weaken from time to time and I would rejoin society with fear of failure. My attention to failure would bring evidence of that into my life.

This process is filled with constant reminders that there is always somewhere for us to grow and expand in consciousness. My business was in its first year, still getting its bearings, and I was finding the natural rhythms of ebb and flow. I had discovered that summer seemed to be a slower season, and I hadn't established enough of a nest egg to cover it. I was in need of $2000 to keep the business running that month. Staying peaceful and centered I thought to myself, "No problem. I can find $2000 easy. I will use The Law of Attraction and it will be drawn to me." I loved challenges like this, opportunities to reestablish my faith in the truth that I am the creator of my life. Mission "find $2000" began. The obvious place to start was the bank. After a couple hours with my favorite banker, I decided we had exhausted all avenues and it was time to look elsewhere. I returned to my business and decided that I had done enough and it was time to get quiet and reconnect. When in doubt, meditate. Something was definitely wrong. I was sensing doors closing; it was feeling too difficult.

Meditation is the key to that gate that is the entry to your heart

Meditation is an opportunity to recalibrate, stop doing and start being. In meditation, you tune into the higher frequency and see if there are any messages that might reveal your next step. Although life is filled with action, you are not the guide. You are the visionary, the artist creating the canvas. This is the time to pull out those paint brushes and empty canvas, place all your desires onto the canvas and hand your completed work of art over to spirit or the universe. Then, let go of the reigns and let the universal spirit be your guide. Sometimes the answer is "Do nothing." But, know that spirit will never rest, hard at work to materialize your desires.

As I quieted my mind from all chatter of the external world, I came back to the simple basics of manifestation. The statement occurred to me, "Where attention goes, energy flows." When I felt those words there was a sense of elation. I created a vision of what those words meant. I saw a tiny spec floating in my mind and imagined as I focused on this spec all the energy of the universe being drawn towards this spec. That is the nature of the universe. Everywhere we look and direct our attention, the universe in all of its vastness is drawn to that thing and its creation. It was so obvious. I had been placing my attention on finding $2000, which was making a statement to the universe that I did not have $2000. I was placing my attention on the lack of. All of the energy in the universe was coming together to create the lack of $2000. It was impossible for the bank to reveal $2000 because that was not where my attention was. I needed to turn my attention in the direction of already having. As I ignored my senses and drew my attention towards the picture of already having the money I needed, the universe had no choice but to reveal that.

With a feeling of relief I had regained my inner peace and reconnected with my sense of well-being and walked to my office. Grabbing a piece of paper, I wrote that statement "Where attention goes, energy flows" so I wouldn't forget again. I knew I already had the $2000. I could wrap all five senses around being in possession of this money. Less than one minute later the postman walked into studio. He handed me one single envelope with a smile. I was smiling too. Even before I saw what he was handing me I knew this was the universe answering my request. I was right. In the envelope was a check for $1877.33. Just thirty minutes later, a woman came in and bought a service for $120.

Now it is time to ask yourself this: "What picture are you seeing and what are you wishing to see?"

~When you release something back into the universe you create a space in your life that the universal law has to fill with something even better~

To understand the need for the universe to reveal what is perceived to be there start with understanding the way Mother Nature insists on filling a hole. Try this for yourself. Dig a hole in your backyard tonight. The law of the universe says that when you wake up in the morning, you will find something in that hole. The universe wants to bestow abundance and prosperity to you. If your closets are full, your hands are closed, and you have filled every second of your day, there is no need left to fill. If you want a new job, new relationship, or more time for yourself to travel, read, or meditate; you must first create an empty space and then ask for the universe to fill it. If you want to bring more of something into your life, you must first make room for it. If you want a new wardrobe, clean out your closet. If you want more money, clean out your wallet. If you want answers, clear out the clutter in your mind. Start to notice whether or not you have created room in your life for what it is that you think you want. You want a relationship, but you hardly have time in your day for the activities you are already involved in. You have to start to make time available and fill it with things that tell the universe you have room for a relationship.

Meditation is the only way to clear your mind to make space for new information. Yoga is considered a moving meditation, an opportunity to find space and move inward, while cleansing your body of build-up and toxins so you can continue to grow and expand, reconnecting with your natural state of being.

Recalibrating Through Meditation:
~What gets in the way of attracting your perfect life?~

Growing aware of your thoughts and becoming a deliberate creator in your life can feel like too much sometimes. When you really start to recognize how many thoughts are running through your mind every day as you process your surroundings, think about yesterday, or plan out tomorrow, it can be overwhelming to try and keep track of it all. Our mind is like a computer. It is taking information in and creating beliefs and then constantly reevaluating all of the information to draw its conclusion.

When we download the earth program at birth, we become susceptible to the earth virus that runs rampant and affects the way we compute our surroundings. Our computers (minds) come with preloaded apps and software that are passed down through our DNA from our parents and grandparents, great grandparents etc.. Before we even open our eyes for the first time, we are programmed with an expectation of what we will see. We might not yet know how to respond to things, but we do have a program installed that allows us to read *other people's* reactions. That helps us form our beliefs about whether or not something is deemed good, bad, or even acknowledged at all.

The apps passed down from your parents to you, may not necessarily be good ones. In fact, you may have started life with an app doomed for failure. Or maybe the cause of the faulty programming is that the wire that connects your computer to the massive networks overlooking all of the computers is loose. This massive network, which can be refer to as god, the universe, all that is, the source, divine, or whatever other word you choose, is what takes your requests, processes them, and makes them your reality. It has no software or apps or filtering system; it is simply the network connecting you to everything.

You can think of this network like the internet. The internet has no biased opinions whatsoever. You place a request in a search engine and it sends you what it thinks you are asking for. Sometimes you have to re-word your request for the right idea to get across and for what you want to show up on the screen. The internet doesn't possess the ability to reason; it takes your request and creates the reality you requested, verbatim. This is why our words are so very important.

Most of us disconnected from source when we were uploaded with the earth virus. If that's the case, when you launch a request via the internet but you're not online or plugged in, how can the request be granted? Without connecting to source you are separated from your divine purpose, your passion, your truth: what you are here to contribute. Without that you cannot be or feel love, happiness, and joy, which is really all your soul wants. Connecting to source is the only cure for the earth virus, and once you plug in it automatically washes your memory clean and reinstalls the program titled "Your true self, the embodiment of love."

~Take time to reconnect with your Higher power~

To reconnect with source all that is necessary is to find

time to sit down and pray, worship, get quiet, or meditate. Go to that place where everything is okay and you feel at peace. Some people practice yoga or visit a church. Being with nature is a wonderful way to find this peace as well. Eventually you will be able to connect with source any place, any time. When you have found your sanctuary, that place where you are surrounded by organic life-giving energy and you can be alone, peaceful and centered, I urge you to go there and try this meditation.

~A meditation to reconnect with source~
Find a few minutes where you will not be interrupted and a quiet place that is clear of burdens or duties. Close your eyes and find a comfortable position, one that takes no effort on your part to support yourself. Feel yourself being supported by the earth beneath you and allow every part of you to let go of resistance and release all tension as you feel the sensation of being supported. At the same time that you find yourself being supported by the earth, recognize the density of your bones and weight of your body as it sinks toward the center of the earth, as if it is being drawn down by a magnet. Feel whatever is directly beneath you, whether the earth, a chair, or a yoga mat, rising off the floor to support you as you sink into it.
Now try to recognize the lightness of your energy, your spirit, as it rises above you toward the heavens, growing lighter and lighter. As your spirit rises above you, imagine it grows brighter, becoming illuminated by a white light which expands the more your spirit moves away from the heaviness of the earth plane and starts to connect you with who you truly are. Become more present into this moment with each passing breath. Feel the breath connecting you to the source of all life as it flows into your lungs, allowing your chest and belly to rise. Notice the sensation of release with the exhale. Notice the release of all earthly burdens flowing out with the breath. With each exhale and

release, imagine your higher self now floating above you becoming lighter, more expanded, and illuminated. The inhale brings light, love, peace, joy. and happiness into the body as the exhale releases anything that is no longer serving you. Find a rhythm in your breaths and continue to notice as the inhale flows up and the exhale moves down.

When you are ready to return to the room and your body, allow that illuminated version of you, the one connected to your truth, flow back into your body. When you are ready, open your eyes.

~ Your Thoughts Have the Ability To Change The World~

The Law of Attraction is fueled by your thoughts. If you want to see something change in your life, start to become aware of your thoughts around that particular thing. Make awareness a high priority. Even if you can't catch the thought as you have it, begin to notice if you can trace events back to thoughts you were having that may have created the events. For example, if you had a fight with your husband, a coworker or friend, when you trace the fight back to its origin, can you recall anticipating the argument or having thoughts about these situations before they occurred? Can you remember a time when you thought "I hope this doesn't happen" and it did? Afterwards, you thought "I knew it!" You were exactly right. You *did* know it. You believed it so much it transpired into your reality. If you would have believed differently the outcome would have changed.

Yes. It really is that easy. Ask for it and then allow it! The universe cannot tell the difference between what you don't want and what you do. It simply hears your request in the form of your thoughts, sees the feelings you are associating with this request, and then delivers what you requested. The intensity and positivity of the feelings you associate with receiving this into your life decides how quickly it will show up. This is why it seems we get more of what we don't want than what we do. It is because we spend a lot of time worrying about what we don't want and very little time wishing about, focusing on, or gaining clarity about what we do want.

The Law of Attraction is far from complex. In fact, it is so simple that we spend most of our time *looking* for the complexity in it. Begin to notice the constant incessant chatter that is happening in your head. Be the observer of your own mind. Our minds are constantly running through play-by-plays of events that have already happened or things we perceive as probable in the future.

As often as you can, try and replace thoughts with low energy words or feelings with those that possess high energy words and feelings. Words like peace, love, joy, happiness, truth, abundance, prosperity, and faith all hold a high vibration. Just saying those words in lieu of words like hate, fear, miserable, dislike, war, or fight can change the way you feel. Changing the way you feel can change the way you think which, in turn, will change the way your life unfolds.

Next time you start to feel depleted, like life is letting you down, try running through a list of uplifting words in your mind or saying them out loud and feel how your energy shifts. A game I often play in the car or through texts with friends is to move through the alphabet one letter at a time. Start with the letter A, and text or say out loud all of the high vibration words that come to mind with that letter. This is a good way to practice.

For example:

    A- Abundance, action, acceptance, affection, amazing.
    B- Beautiful, brilliant, bountiful, bliss, believe, become
    C- Caring, considerate, calm, compassion

Words hold power. Try replacing the phrases "I wish," "I would," or "I can" with "I will." Never say "I can't." Instead, say "I choose not to." These are powerful movements in the direction of becoming a deliberate creator and not just someone who stands by and lets the world happen to them.

~What do you want?~

As a group, The Power of Light, was ready to start testing the theories we were discussing. We were ready to decide our future and take responsibility for our past in a supportive group setting. Knowing it is easier to stop the limiting beliefs in someone else we vowed to hold each other accountable. We spent weeks fine tuning our manifesting skills, studying and gathering information. Together, we worked on manifestation and visualization meditations, positive thinking, and becoming aware of our thoughts, and we began to notice things we hadn't before. We felt we were ready to do something big and use our knowledge in the classroom of life.

I had asked everyone in the group to bring a description of what their perfect life would look like to the next meeting. I had encouraged them to get creative, to go to that place that has been deemed impossible to achieve due to life circumstances and describe what that life would look like. This was when I discovered the biggest and most important truth: the first step on the path to realizing your dreams is revealing what your dreams are!

Over the Rainbow

Here is the worksheet they did:

Chapter Seventeen
Worksheet

Before writing your list down, clear your mind and remove all reality from it. This is not a rational thinking exercise. This is an exercise in dreaming as if the possibilities were endless.

Go to that place in you where all of your dreams exist, that place buried somewhere deep in the back of your mind under piles of why they can't ever be true. Pretend that you stand in front of a giant pot filled with ALL THAT IS, and that you have been given permission to reach into that pot and pull out anything that your heart desires! It is all right there in the pot of infinite possibilities. There are absolutely no restrictions or limitations on what you can ask for. Now, I ask you: what are you going to pull out? Answer the questions below as though you were already living this life.

* *describe your relationships with those close to you. These relationships may include your family, friends, coworkers etc. (remember that these relationships may not exist yet. I.e. if you are looking for your soulmate, how would they add to your life?) Use an extra sheet if you need to*
* *Where are you living? Why? How does this space fulfill you?*
* *What does each day look like as far as day-to-day activities? What do you do with your free time? What are your hobbies? What would you do if you had endless resources?*
* *How do you see yourself touching the lives of those around you?*

Over the Rainbow

Section Three
Destination…
Dreams Come True.

~How will you ever get there if you keep staying here?~

~Are you just going through the motions every day?

~Do you know your passions and purpose in life?

~Expand your perceptions to see something greater.

Over the Rainbow

CHAPTER EIGHTEEN
~*How To Discover Your Purpose*~

When the group returned the next week, with their worksheets, I expected a new excitement in the air as we shared our deepest desires, dreams, goals, and aspirations. I was excited to hear the wishes of the people I had grown so close to over the past year. And, even more excited to use these laws and watch their dreams become their reality.

We gathered in a circle and prepared to share. As each person ran down their list I couldn't help but wonder if they had even read the instructions for filling out the worksheet. One by one they took the podium and restated the life they were already living with a little more flare. They had been told to dream without limits, and they were describing the same house with an extra bedroom. They were told to describe their perfect relationships, and they all said they were satisfied in their current relationships…if only their significant other would stop doing this or that or if their children would make more time for them in their lives, or if their mom and dad could have a nice evening as family and all get along. They said everyone around them was perfect just as they were…if only they wouldn't treat them this way or that. I was standing there with a wand, waiting to grant any of their wishes, but there were no wishes to grant!

These people were showing up every week to a group designed to manifest the life they wanted. I had to assume that there was *something* missing in their current circumstances. They were looking for more; they just didn't know what. At that point it became crystal clear why they hadn't already received it! *They didn't know what "it" was!* They were stuck in the state of looking for more, but the path to actually having more wasn't even visible because they didn't know what they wanted. Without the knowledge of what their ideal "dream" life looked like, how would they recognize it if it was right outside their door?

The seed that I had planted long ago finally escaped the shadow of the beliefs, limitations and blocks that had been shading it from light and sprung up into a beautiful garden of endless possibilities fueled by passion and directed by purpose. The group heard the limitation in each other and began to ask questions and dispel limiting beliefs or untruths and eventually we would filter through all the muck and reveal the gem they had forgotten existed. That little thing that lit up their soul at one time but they buried under the "Why not's."

As they released their blocks the dreams became their reality. One woman finally revealed in a meek voice her dreams of being a dancer. As people became very supportive and digging for more information, she opened up. She said, she used to dance and perform and she misses it a lot but, her family needed her around and it was taking up too much time. She mentioned her husband was always jealous and it caused a lot of friction in their marriage. I asked her if she could image it differently. If she was able to imagine her husband sitting in the audience as her number one fan. She became enraged at the ridiculousness of that. It was absolutely impossible and that was that! As she was leaving that night I stopped her at the door and asked the entire group to tell her on a scale of one to ten, from an outside perspective how attainable was her dream? Everyone emphatically answered ten! People were saying she could just take lessons or dance in her home.

I love this story because in embraces a truth that is available to all of us. *We* are the only thing ever holding us back from living our dreams. The next week she returned to the group and told everyone she had created a studio out of one of her spare rooms. As now her children were older and moved out. As the weeks passed she continued on her journey just taking the steps as they revealed themselves. Less than 6 months later she was performing professionally and now she is a sought after performer. To top it off, recently I saw something she had posted on facebook thanking her husband for being her number one fan!

True happiness resides outside the realm of fear.

Fear doesn't exist anymore when you are living your truth. Life becomes an expression of love. Your work transforms into an expression of joy, enthusiasm, and happiness. Your relationships are no longer based on the fear that no one better will love you, or the fear of loneliness. Every relationship is an honest expression of love and you only create relationships that feed and nourish your spirit, catapulting you into a greater version of self. Your relationships will begin to reflect your wants, your wishes and your dreams.

We have a tendency to encapsulate ourselves into the life that we have created, with no room for what we want to find its way in. You must expand the circle around you to create room for more to fit. A magnificent example of expansion is this story of a client I once had. She was a single woman in search of the love of her life and was transitioning into a new area with a new job, searching for a new home. She purchased a five-bedroom house with hopes that someday she would have a big family that would fill all of the rooms. The home she purchased started as dirt and a picture provided by the builder. She had the ability to create her manifestation from the ground up. She took great care in every decision she made, keeping her big vision in mind in every aspect of the house. She would say things like, "I imagine my husband would want a nicely lit garage to work in" or "I want two sinks in the master so my husband will have his own space and I will have mine." If I didn't already know she was single, I would have believed that she was already married.

Sure enough, the beautiful perfection of The Law of Attraction came to her aid as it can be no other way. A year later I received a call. She was scheduling her honeymoon. She knew that all she had to do was ask and believe, and the universe has to deliver. And it did.

Most of us don't want to announce what we hope will happen because we don't truly have the faith that it will. Each time we announce, it we feel badly inside as we are confirming that it is something we don't already have. She had a fearless faith and rejoiced each time she talked about her home filled with a loving family.

When we are still living in fear, the miserable that we know is always more comfortable than the thought of how the unknown might fail us.

It *isn't* the thought of all the rooms filled with a large, happy, loving family that we are afraid of. It is the thought, "what if we never find that significant other and are never able to fill those rooms?" Fear of the disappointment keeps you from having faith, anticipation and expansion. It is easier and safer this way, you tell yourself. Anything else would entail change, and change would be venturing into the unknown...and the unknown is scary. This is the virus speaking.

When you turn to love, you see nothing but the endless possibilities of the unknown and that feeling of fear turns into a tinge of excitement for what could be. For most, there is a fear associated with even thinking about the unknown. It is intrinsic to our nature to turn towards fear in the face of the unknown simple because it *is* unknown. Our mind can't process it and tell us we are safe, because the mind has never been here before. This is when you have to turn to your heart for guidance. Reassure the mind that you have heard its concerns and, as the mind feel comforted and begins to quiet down, turn to your heart for the answers.

~The Unknown~
What would you do differently today if you knew you wouldn't fail? This is a difficult question if you are searching your mind for the answer, because, the answer resides in your heart!

You have only two ways that you can view the unknown. The first is with an optimism and faith that it will bring all that you desire. This is the road least traveled. Only a few brave souls are able to view the unknown this way. These are our pioneers and leaders, the people that change our world. They view things from a perspective that they can't fail.

This was what I was looking for in those worksheets. I wanted each person in the group to tell me what they would do if they knew it couldn't and wouldn't fail. Imaging they possessed magical powers and any of their wishes would be granted immediately no matter how outlandish they were. Wishes are the seeds of an optimism tree. Without the possibility of magic and miracles, life becomes dull, boring, and disappointing. With wishes grow possibility, vision, dreams, and faith.

Faith is something that you use every day whether you realize it or not. Some of you may test faith regularly with large leaps off a cliff with no lifeline or parachute. You know that you will grow wings and fly before you hit the ground. Those people, like super heroes, stamp a giant "F" on their chest and allow faith to create the life of their dreams. They recognize *faith* as the only thing that stands between them and their dreams.

Their dreams and visions have consistently fed their optimism trees with water and sunlight until these trees grew far above the clouds, never to be shaded again. The optimism tree makes someone so strong that they will knock down everything that stands in their way and, in faith, open a new business serving the community with love and passion or design new, innovative technology nobody else could have dreamed possible. These are the people that will drop everything and give up all that they have to move to a foreign land away from family and friends. They understand that the size of their faith determines the size of their magical powers.

Remember my experience in the 8X8 jail cell. I was told a similar story of an 8x8 room being a stop on the way to someone revealing the life of their dreams. A young, charming entrepreneur had a vision of making the world a better place one email at a time. He started a website and committed to sending a daily message of love and well-being to anyone who signed up to receive it. These messages were gentle reminders that you are loved and gushed with inspiration. A year after launch he had established investors and a following of close to 1000 people. Just when things were looking up, it all came crumbling down. In the space of one week he watched his whole foundation disintegrate. His girlfriend broke up with him, his roommates moved out, leaving a rent much too large to manage alone and his investors pulled out of the website. Scrambling to keep it together he moved into a small garage at the back of a friend's house. The garage was an 8x8 living space. He sat on his bed the first night looking at this room and feeling defeated, and asked god why? He said "why the 8x8 room? What are you trying to tell me?" As soon as he launched the question the answer arrived. The response was "The 8x8 room signifies the size of your faith. If you want more you must first expand your faith." That moment he saw it was up to him. He went to sleep that night and when he woke in the morning Kim Kardashian had tweeted that everyone should check out his website and sign up for a daily email. By morning he had 10,000 followers. What is the size of your faith?

You are these people. You already possess what it takes to conquer the world if necessary in pursuit of realizing your dreams.

Faith can also be used on a small scale every single day. What are you going to do today? It takes faith to get in your car and drive to work. You are trusting that you will safely arrive at your destination. Even walking down the stairs or leaving your home takes a small amount of faith. We all get in airplanes from time to time, or step out onto a crosswalk and trust we will be safe. Faith is the only way to get things done. If you allow one thought of fear to infiltrate your thoughts of accomplishing the goal, that single thought holds the power to diminish your super powers. Fear is how societies crumble. Fear can weaken even the most solid foundations.

When you are not in faith, you are in fear. This is very common. There is no middle ground. You are either moving forward with faith that it will all be okay or you are stagnant in fear that you will do something wrong so you don't move at all. In fear, the mind suddenly becomes inundated with thoughts of *what if,* or *I should be satisfied with where I am.* Those thoughts are much easier for most of us than thoughts of happiness or joy, of stepping into newness and having it all work out perfectly.

The media, our parents, and our teachers have all trained us to be cautious: Don't step into the unknown, don't trust anyone. These are the messages that we have been told throughout our lives. This is NOT merely a survival instinct! It is not the brain's default position! Have those thoughts ever saved you in an unsafe situation? No! They have only prevented you from experiencing life to its fullest potential.

What if you could reprogram your brain to only see visions of everything working out perfectly? What if your mind sent out an alarm only when there is a step that is necessary to take *right now*? I am here to tell you that it can happen! It starts with recognizing when those thoughts of fear or failure arise, and then turning them around to thoughts of all your dreams unfolding perfectly, with everything working out in ways you do not have the ability to see right now!

You were probably fearful about getting on the plane your first time. Your mind might have said that giant machines made of metal shouldn't fly. Maybe this was your first vacation away from home. You visualized your destination, took time to carefully plan it out. You looked at different hotels and imagined what each one would look like and what your experience might be like once you were there. You thought carefully about your destination and how it would allow you to relax, unwind, and see new places and things. Now is the day of departure and you are experiencing your first moment of fear. You could have let that fearful feeling stop you from getting on the plane, just like you allow it to interject into every other part of your life, stopping you from taking that risk with the grand payoff. The difference is, you looked around and saw that everyone else believes this plane can fly too, and you jumped onto faith with the collective consciousness. You, of course, arrived safely and were able to experience expansion as you ventured to a new land and saw new things and new experiences, just as you had imagined. Now, imagine what it would have felt like if you had let the fear stop you.

You were designed to be in a constant state of expansion. Stagnancy and contraction diminish your light and your spirit and your desire to be alive. The world needs you to shine brightly. You are a creator, creating all day, every day, with your thoughts and feelings. Whether or not you directly experience or see these manifestations you are adding to the world. You are a part of the collective consciousness.

Collective consciousness did not always agree that airplanes could fly. It took pioneers with undeniable faith to make it widely accepted. The story of the first airplane is a beautiful example of the power of choosing to live in faith, not fear. Imagine the level of impenetrable faith that the Wright brothers had as they not only built but then flew the first plane. They had to believe with such intensity that they were able to convince everyone else it was possible, too. When people tried to convince them that they were crazy, they had to stay so firm in their beliefs that they were able to, just for a minute, make everyone watching want to believe, too.

When you are in faith with a vision, you are enthusiastic. Enthusiasm is a fuel and it is contagious. It can make anything possible. The Wright brothers started with a small aircraft. Now we have massive passenger aircrafts, and as people hop on there is no question as whether or not it is possible. But without the original faith, it never would have happened.

~All answers need a question~

If the new goal for my group involved taking a step back and getting the group clear on what they wanted before we could start to design and create our lives, then I had to find a way to get people dreaming again. You can't ask for something outside of your spectrum of knowledge. This is why expansion is tricky. If you have never seen or heard of something, than you can't know what it would feel like to have it! That makes it very unlikely that you would be able to request it.

We watch movies and look at magazines to try and expand, imagining what it would feel like to have or experience what we are viewing. This is good because it gives us experiences to grow from. However, this isn't your final destination on the path to your dreams being realized, because when we watch a movie, we feel the particular feeling the person that created the visual experience wants us to feel. So you may dream this thing into your life, associating this thing with that feeling you were guided into having, and realize in that your actual life experience it doesn't feel anything like you had imagined.

We encourage our children to imagine and dream outside the spectrum of reality, but by adolescence you are expected to let go of the imaginary world and take hold of the world that society presents to you. Society guides us with movies and television shows, books detailing the prescription to joy. The basic message is…if you have a relationship, home, job, and friends, then you are happy. So you stay in this constant state of searching for your happiness through those things. You think, maybe this isn't the right relationship because I'm not happy yet. You think if you change your friends' behavior or find new friends altogether, they will hold the key to your happiness. But when you visit your heart, you know that there is something more to life. You have always known.

I urge you to separate for a moment and close your eyes, get quiet, and visit your heart. That is where the true key to your happiness lies. It is where you go when everything is still and you just connect with you. It is in your heart that you will discover your true passion and purpose. Your heart reminds you that you hold the answer, the key to the universe in your hand. Everything is always unfolding perfectly, exactly as it should.

You may ask, "If this is so, why do I see people suffering? Why are there homeless people who are hungry and hurt?" Without exception, life delivers to you exactly what you ask it to. This applies to the homeless as well. They have their journey and purpose and they are fulfilling it perfectly. It is only your perception that views it as suffering. To them, it is just another day. They haven't expanded beyond that life or asked for anything different.

Imagine stepping into a third world country. The bathrooms don't have soap, running water, or even toilet paper most of the time. The areas for food preparation are very unsanitary. People are living in conditions that you would deem miserable and you feel sadness for their suffering. But they are laughing and playing and appreciative of the little things. They do not know what you have decided they are missing. How can they dream or wish for something that they have never encountered or seen? They don't have access to books, television, movies. They are not longing for those things to notice their lack. We feel uncomfortable in those situations because we are experiencing the contrast of what we have come to know as comfort.

Your mind doesn't hold the answer to what are your deepest desires, because the answer lies in the limitless possibilities of creation found in your heart.

The quickest route to arrive in your heart and connect with your spirit is dreaming. Invoking the inner child that loved to splatter paint on an empty canvas and imagine it to be a beautiful masterpiece. You didn't need the world to tell you what they saw, you saw it even when they couldn't.

It can be difficult for us to quiet down the programming that is in our minds. Even in the stillness, our brains can tap into radio waves or frequencies all around us. Have you ever had a song flowing through your mind, and when you turned on the radio that song is playing at the exact place you were hearing it? This is because you were tapping into those radio waves that are present all around us, all of the time. The sounds that can't be heard by the conscious mind but, the subconscious mind hears loud and clear! These sounds can create thoughts you may have never had. So, ask yourself from time to time "Are these even my thoughts I am having? Is this me speaking in my mind? Do I really feel this way, or do I choose to have different thoughts that are born of *MY* heart?"

Quieting the mind takes a lot of practice, discipline and determination. You can start by directing your thoughts to visions that bring good sensations into your body. This begins to harness your mind and move it in the direction of awareness.

As you begin this process of escaping from reality to expand your realm of possibilities, you may experience guilt

162

or shame. When you daydream about possible alternate futures, you can feel unappreciative for the people and things you have in your life right now. It is natural to feel bad as though wishing for something else says that what you currently have isn't good enough. I urge you to love what you have! Count your blessing every day, and look for gratitude in every situation. If you are not experiencing gratitude for what you have, you are denying The Law of Attraction and saying that life isn't working to your favor. What you have and what you want are there to reveal to you the contrast. They keep you expanding and they keep fine-tuning your wish list. As you experience what you *don't* want, look for the contrast and daydream about already having what you *do* want. What you fail to recognize is that it is all just one big dream anyway.

"So long as the dreamer dreams, dream-objects are real. When he wakes up, the dream world becomes false. When one attains illumination or knowledge of Brahman, this wakeful world becomes as unreal as the dream world." The Vedas

There is a common Sanskrit word, *maya*, which loosely translates to *illusion*. Sanskrit is the language used in yoga studios all over the world to describe the *asanas* (postures), the breath, and the ascension into the connection of mind, body, and spirit. Sanskrit is used instead of English because these words have a very high vibration. The sounds produced when speaking this language resonate with the frequency of creation. It is one of the oldest languages recorded. Sanskrit words are packed with so much power we find ourselves writing a small book to translate into English the meaning intended in just one Sanskrit word. Therefore, we do not have an English word that can accurately portray what the sages/masters meant when they used the word *maya*. When you hear that word, you must experience its meaning for yourself. When you have awakened to a vision of life beyond *maya* (illusion) for even a moment, you will be able to grasp the intended meaning of this word.

We are taught that we are irresponsible if we spend our time dreaming about the impossible instead of staying in the *real world*. We are told that if we don't spend all of our time preparing for the disaster that is sure to happen, we will experience suffering. However, a person who spends their life this way is *already* living a life of self-induced and unnecessary suffering. The person who recognizes this, and experiences life in general, as *maya* will dance and play through life. They won't care what society thinks of them and they will live their life to the fullest enjoyment with no regrets. A person who has awakened to this truth is like someone waking from a nightmare in which they are running for their life. Upon awakening, you realize that it was all *maya*, illusion. There never was someone chasing you. It did not exist. Nevertheless, being an illusion does not make it unreal. The experience you had while running for life was absolutely real while the dream was occurring. You may even wake in a sweat or breathing hard. Yet, through the clarity of wakefulness, you see that the dream was not real.

What makes the dream world "fake" and the waking world "real?" There is no objective experiment we can run to prove that the waking state we are in right now is any more real than last night's dream, which also felt completely real. Treat your life like a dream you get to create moment by moment.

There is a parable that describes this perfectly. The story begins with a King named Janaka. He had dreamt that he was a beggar being persecuted by a group of villagers. They had thrown him onto the ground and were beating him with their fists, throwing stones and handfuls of dirt at him. Suddenly, he awoke. There he was, King Janaka, adorned with silk and jewels, being fanned by servants in his luxurious castle. Shocked by the contrast, he closed his eyes and fell immediately back into the dream, where the villagers were still beating him as he cowered on the ground in fear for his life. Once again, he awoke, finding himself in the lap of luxury. This happened twice more. Janaka was fascinated and intrigued by the experience. Both states felt equally real when he was in them. How, then, could he know which one was true and which was *maya*, illusion? Was he the beggar or the king?

Back in the waking state, King Janaka called in all of his wise prime ministers and advisors, and asked them which state was real. None were able to answer the question to his satisfaction. In the meantime, a young son of a sage stepped into the courtyard. He was crippled, and made quite a spectacle of himself as he hobbled down the aisle to the throne. Many of the townsfolk who had gathered laughed at what they saw as a ridiculous figure. The boy knelt down before the king, and with great effort stood back up. "Your Majesty, I have come to answer your question."

Now the bystanders were whispering and chuckling under their breath. This kid was surely asking for trouble. But, the king saw a light around the boy's face, and was guided by deep intuition to allow him to say his piece, even though it seemed unlikely that this boy would ever be able to answer the question.

"Fine," said the King, intrigued. "Tell me which state is real, the waking state or the dream state?"

The young boy replied, "O King. Neither the waking

state nor the dream states are real. Only the Self is real, the Self that is beyond all *maya*."

"The phenomena of life can be compared to a dream, a ghost, an air bubble, a shadow, glittering dew, the flash of lightning, and must be contemplated as such."Buddha

What is revealed right now as your day-to-day life is a reflection of what you expect, either from watching what others around you are experiencing or what you feel you deserve. Expectations have been being molded since they day you were born. For the most part, what you see as your life today is what you learned to expect from watching those around you as a child.

You have the misconception that you are more in control of creating your reality when you are stating all of the things that you don't want to happen and not leaping outside the box you have learned to expect. You think that stating these *negative expectations* out loud somehow prepares your psyche to handle this worst case scenario. It protects your ego as well. You can always say "I knew it would happen." Or, if it works out better than predicted, there is no harm to the ego at all. However, it cannot work out better than predicted unless the expectation is set for this desired outcome. It is a catch twenty-two.

Maybe you tried this faith-based approach and told everyone you encountered that something great was going to happen. You said it with confidence and sounded very convincing, but you didn't really believe it. In that case, you would see and believe with ease the evidence that verified you were not speaking the truth. You may even feel a sense of relief when it doesn't happen, because that was your true expectation all along. You set yourselves up to feel satisfied with life unfolding as a series of disappointments that you can pat yourself on the back for being smart enough to have expected.

This scenario is the mind's way of maintaining control. Your mind wants to be proven right so you can faithfully rely on your mind to predict the outcome of events. This is reassuring and comforting, even if it means that we remain in misery. In other words, while preparing for the worst brings some level of satisfaction and security, it brings no level of joy and happiness.

Joy is never found in the mind. Joy and happiness are only ever found when the mind is silent and you blindly follow your heart.

The dream sheets I had received from the group directly reflected this concept. We all possess our stories, the stories we have been telling for lifetimes. It is very hard to let go of these stories as they have defined who we are. These stories tell of our hardships and how we have fought and worked to achieve what we have. We have to let go of our stories and begin to tell new stories of life working perfectly and how we always get what we ask for immediately upon request.

I am your genie, your wish is my command

Let go of your stories… So you can create the fairytale

I noticed, when people were discussing what they didn't want they did it with confidence, energy, and strong negative feelings attached to it. Asking for something and attaching feelings to the asking, forces the universe into compliance. Most people's experience is of the universe revealing to them what they didn't want based on that being where their attention is placed. You can always bet on the fact that what you are saying out loud is where your attention, energy and focus is. Everyone is guilty of drawing more of what we don't want into our lives by creating and telling stories to invoke a certain feeling in those we are telling.

My now ex-husband often drank incapacitating amounts when we were out with his friends. Having grown up with an addict I had a strong distaste for this behavior. Habit became expectation and eventually I came to rely on him to drink too much and portray the same destructive behavior I had come to know too well from a life surrounded by drugs.

It was not just the story I was telling about him, but the story I was also telling about myself that created the outcome I was running from. It is easy to get stuck on the hamster wheel, replaying over and over again one scene from your life, in which your role is the victim. Just like the movie "Groundhogs Day", my life would continue to show up the exact same way as long as that was the story I was telling. I would tell everyone that would listen, how awful it was for me to go out with him. Telling the story of how I felt like he didn't care about me or respect my wishes when he would get that intoxicated. I would also cast these poisoned words his way.

We can hold people hostage in a role they are expected to play in our life by seeing them only as their failures. I would tell anyone that would listen, including him, that he had a problem with alcohol and needed to get help! People that are closely attached to you have the ability to affect your reality with their thoughts about you, as I did him. I would have assisted both me and my husband simply by seeing him as someone who is responsible when he drinks and has all of his priorities in the right place. Seeing the truth; what is left without the stories.

I know this is not easy! Denying all that you know is like lying to yourself. You have seen, smelled, touched, felt and believed something that is very real to you. How can I imagine and connect all five of my senses to another story? This is when I urge you to pull out your empty canvas. Erase all that you know and start from scratch creating your masterpiece.

There are two realities, one we create in our minds and the one we experience when our eyes open? To change your reality, you must choose the one you create in your mind. I needed to be able to disregard what my senses told me and created for myself the dream in which my husband would never, *and has never,* behaved in such a way. Then I would need to shift my belief to this dream, and not to what my senses tell me is reality. The trick lies in changing your perception of reality.

"What if you slept? And what if, in your sleep, you went to heaven and there plucked a strange and beautiful flower? And what if, when you awoke, you had the flower in your hand? Ah, what then?" Samuel Taylor Coleridge

Doesn't it just make sense that changing the way we think, will change the way we speak, and we might spend more time connecting with a higher vision of those we love and our own lives? Start to see everyone around you living as their highest self, even if there is absolutely no evidence of this ever happening. When you are cultivating a new story for yourself, cultivate a new story you tell about your loved ones as well. This is the simple key to living your life with passion and on purpose. Knowing what you want and recognizing that everyone, fundamentally, wants much of the same. We are all looking for love, happiness, joy, passion, expansion. All of those things are found in the answer to one simple question. What do you want?

Yoga is referred to as a practice because the mat is a place where you return to yourself and the self is ever expanding and evolving. Therefore, the practice of yoga is ever changing for the practitioner and different for everyone. And always allows for a deeper understanding of self.

At one point I remember feeling stuck. I wondered if I had maximized the potential of my body. Having watched so many other yogis that didn't possess nearly as much physical strength or dedication as myself and seemed to float through their practice, flying into the air with ease and a sense of grace I decided it was possible. Through determination and a decision that the answer was out there, I just hadn't found it yet, I encountered one master teacher who possessed the magical words I had been searching for. And it was simple. She said, "If you want to know how to master the art of flowing through inversions with ease, you must simply change your relationship with gravity."

I knew then that the answer would be found once I analyzed what relationship I held with gravity. For starters, I knew that life had showed me gravity demands my feet be on the ground for me to find balance. When I carefully considered this belief about gravity, the vision of a baby being born to a family that walks on their hands appeared. I thought to myself that surely the baby would begin to walk on his hands as well and probably do it with ease. Then, later in his life, if someone wanted him to walk on his feet, it would likely be a very uncomfortable experience. My beliefs about gravity played a role in my life, whether I realized it or not. When I changed those expectations and looked for the root of the belief disproving it, viola, Like magic, I greatly deepened my practice of inversions.

If you encounter situations that involve your expectations or conditioning from your past, and you find yourself in fear of life turning out like you expect it to, try changing your expectations. What is the worst that could happen? Setting an intention for my evening with my ex-husband would have stopped the freight train from coming and completely changed the outcome of that evening all together. People can only live up to what you expect of them. Setting an intention would have been an opportunity to realign myself with what I *did* want, allowing the universe to deliver the perfect experience to bring the desired feelings.

Over the Rainbow

CHAPTER NINETEEN
~*How to Ask for What You Want*~

When asking for what you want, you must phrase it with words that reflect your hearts desires. In other words, you can't just say, "I don't want to argue," because the universe only hears and sees "argue," and then sets into motion a plan to give you more of that. Whatever you are thinking, feeling, picturing and saying is what the universe responds to. If you don't want to argue, you must think, feel, and say, "I want peace and love."

This takes practice: Not just practicing the manipulation of thoughts, but practicing the cultivation of the feelings attached to the thoughts. We have all developed a way of thinking and feeling. Many of us have spent our whole lives focused on the "fight against something" mentality: we have the *War on Drugs, Mothers Against Drunk Driving*, the *War on Terrorism*. It is the way the massive consciousness works. We are now at a crossroads where it is up to you to change the overall consciousness that is plaguing the earth. You alone hold this power. Begin to state things in the affirmative. Make people aware of what they are really asking for when they say they support the "war" on drugs: They are asking for a war. What if, instead, they supported people living life substance-free? Both say the same thing, but which one feels better when said or heard? The fight *against* something brings more of that something into our awareness. It keeps giving us what we are fighting *against* so that we can keep fighting.

Here's how those phrases would read if we were state them under this system: *Living Life Sober and Free, Healthy, and Happy, Mothers for Child Safety, Standing for Peace.*

In this technology-driven society, we all have either a computer or a smart phone or both. The smart phones are programmed to recognize patterns and words that you have a tendency to use. As you start typing, it tries to finish your statement based on these patterns and tendencies. You are typing "I love you, Steve," but the phone remembers your last boyfriend and tries to fill in the name "Bob" instead. Now you have the opportunity to double check your text, change it to what it should read, and send it…or to send it without catching the mistake. This is exactly how the brain works. It recognizes patterns and will fill in the blanks to complete your thoughts before you have the opportunity to redirect them. This is why you must practice catching your thoughts and redirecting them.

The mind is flexible, and can be retrained. Eventually, the more your brain sees the name "Steve" instead of "Bob," it will learn. It will place the correct name in your subconscious so you will automatically arrive at it whenever you say the words "I love you." It takes awareness and practice, but you *can* develop new ways of thinking.

~We Choose Lack to Avoid Guilt or Judgment~

In most situations, when people are forced to state what they *do* want, they often become fearful of being judged so they choose their words carefully, stumbling over how to state what they want without sounding greedy or ungrateful. Even if their soul is secretly wishing for something, they are scared to tell the world because they have relied on the world for feedback. And the response has been, "You don't deserve that! What makes you think you are so special?"

You don't want people to think badly about you because there are others out there suffering without food and clothing. Why should you get everything your heart desires while others are suffering with sickness and poverty? The answer is; that their suffering is their path of choice and it is only suffering from where you stand through your goggles of perception. In their eyes it is just another day. Somewhere in the world, somebody may even be in a place of perspective where they can see your life and feel sorry for you in your pain and suffering, while to you it is just another day.

The world has told you, "You have to work hard for your money, and even then, there is rarely enough to go around." You expect to see lack and suffering. If it isn't you who is experiencing lack then it has to be somebody so you look until you see it and confirm the belief once again. The key to happiness is simple. The universe does not care whether you are asking to verify that your life is full of riches or asking to verify that you never have enough. You get to choose the thought, and whichever one you pick and start to believe is the one that will start to show up in your life time and time again. It is only your responsibility to feel good as often as you can so you can.

~Why Do We Stay Here, When What We Want is Over There?~

If we can't ask for what we want clearly and believe that we deserve it, while remaining open and willing to receive it when it arrives, how can it ever come to be? There *is* enough abundance to go around! The more on purpose and passionate we are living, the stronger our influence on the world around us. When abundance and prosperity is filling you up, you are able to lovingly decide where to direct this abundance as you cycle it back through society.

Anything that you ever see or hear that brings you to thoughts of lack, fear, anger, guilt is a lie! Write that down so you never forget it. Fear and lack do not exist, they are imagined. You are fine right now, no matter what is happening. You have enough. Fear and lack are the projection of an imagined future and bringing those feelings into this moment because of an imagined future will never serve you. Mass consciousness will tell you that, *because it was what you were already thinking*. If you started thinking differently and announced it to the world, very different messages would come back at you to verify your new thoughts.

If you love what you do, you more often than not, live a meager existence. It feels wrong to expect to make a lot of money doing something you love. Even performers get seduced by this belief and will do projects not born of their heart because "you can't always do what you love and make money". Society looks at those doing good, who are happy and love what they do, and decides that they should stay within a means that is a notch above struggle or just enough. This is because as a society we have decided money comes from work and work is something you have to do. The more you dislike what you do, the more you should be paid! People have a hard time mingling the love of their work with the evil that is money and materialism. Priests, teachers, charities and nonprofits those people who we see as doing good for the betterment of all are frowned upon if they are seen driving a car that's too flashy or living in a house that is too big. We are here to recognize all of the limiting beliefs and become an inspiration for the world to follow guiding a new way of life in which limitation does not exist and the possibilities are as limitless as your imagination.

~3 Wishes, No Limits...~

Do you know what you want? I mean do you *really* know what you want? If this book came with a magic genie ready to grant you three wishes, do you know what you would wish for? Take out your notebook right now and write down three wishes. They can be anything. Once you write them down, tear out that page and use it as your bookmark while reading through the rest of these pages, so you can keep these wishes close to you while your heart is opening to infinite possibilities. The truth is, you *do* have a magical genie and he *is* waiting to grant *all* of your wishes with *no* limits.

Finding your magic brings back the wonder and beauty that you once saw as a child. Your whole world opens up and you become creative and inspired once again. Imagination and creativity are muscles that need to be exercised. As adults our lives become very boxed in and routine, we rarely stretch outside of what we expect to see, so our imagination and creation center in our brains shrinks from lack of use. Wishing, praying, dreaming and believing all begin to strengthen this part of your brain. Once again you will find the eyes of a child accessible to you, and you will see wonder and magnificence everywhere.

Learning the language of the universe reconnects you with enthusiasm, happiness, and joy. Enthusiasm is infectious. People will become drawn to you and your cause, because they want what you have. Not the stuff or possessions, but the excitement for life and the eyes of a child. When your spark gets ignited and starts to shine brighter, people are drawn to you like moths to a flame. Enthusiasm literally translates as *"A God Within" inspiration from or possession by the divine or God*. The more people who can see your vision the more power your vision will hold.

~Careful What You Wish For~

When writing down your wishes, be careful what you wish for. We all heard this many times growing up. For a moment consider whether or not you ever really thought about the power of those words. Our thoughts are creation at its conception, and it is so much easier to direct our thoughts in a way that defines our truth if we take a moment to get clear on what it is we want. Listen to the words in your wish very carefully. Look for any ways you are settling or minimizing. Are you clear enough with your wish that a genie who can't see inside your mind would be able to, from your description, grant your wish exactly the way you want it? Think about those wishes you wrote down, take your time, get clear. Ask yourself: is this really what I want. If I had this right now, would it make me happy?

~Why Meditate?~

The most important step in asking for what you want is to believe you already have it. Get a clear picture of whatever it is you would like to manifest in your life. Meditation is a very important part of learning to create what you want. You have to learn to quiet the mind to minimize the influence of the outside world on the truth of what your highest self wants to realize in this lifetime.

In the space of quiet, we are able to cultivate a true and deep connection with the divine. This connection will reveal to you what you really want. As you visualize, you bring the experience into the body as if it is actually happening. You begin to bring it from the dream world into the real world. That is the creative power of manifestation!

~Visualization~

A recent study at Bishop's University in Canada revealed that the power of visualization in the mind can make matching gains in weight loss and strength without exerting any energy! The study involved three different groups of people. These people, for the sake of the study, agreed to measure their strength gains over a period of time. Each group was told to do something different to achieve their results: Group one, the control group, changed absolutely nothing from their regular routine; group two was put through two weeks of highly focused strength training; group three was instructed to listen to audio compact discs that took them through the same exercise routine as group two, but not to do the workouts.

The results were astonishing to say the least. The control group, who changed nothing in their routine, saw no change in their strength or weight. The exercise group saw a 28% increase in their strength. This was of course, expected, and did nothing to change our current perception of life that says you must physically strain and work hard to receive the results you want.

However, what happened to group three proved that the power of our mind absolutely has the ability to create our reality. Group three saw a 24% increase in strength, almost identical to that of the group that actually did the workouts! Merely listening to and visualizing the workout had the same effect as doing it!

This is not the only study with results like these. Numerous other studies have been conducted where groups of people are hooked up to machines designed to recognize when certain muscles in the body are firing. These people were told to watch videos where they are placed in the driver's seat of a race car. As the car moves around the track, the muscles in the person's body fire as if they were actually driving a race car.

If the brain and the body cannot tell the difference between what is actually happening and what you are visualizing, it makes sense that you should spend time visualizing what you want. Daydream! Allow your dreams to transform your reality. Here is a guided meditation that will help you improve your ability to visualize and move towards unlimited thinking. It might be helpful to either have someone read this to you while you sit, or record yourself reading it first. Then find a place where you will be undisturbed for at least ten minutes and listen to it.

Meditation by: Sanaya Roman(Orin and DaBen)
I allow myself to relax, releasing all tension and stress.
I find a comfortable position
and allow my shoulders to release down and back as I gently
exhale.
I allow my legs, thighs, and feet to soften.
I inhale peace, love, joy and truth.
I exhale resistance and stagnancy.
I soften the muscles supporting my eyes and my jaw.
I use the exhale to sink deeper.
I let go of the need to do anything
so that I can breathe
more easily and deeply.
I allow my mind to become clear.
It is like a clear mountain lake
that reflects the light above.
My mind clearly reflects
the unlimited thinking
of my Higher Self, the peace in
Knowing who I really am.
I imagine my mind becoming
brilliant and insightful.
I say to myself,
"I am open to the new.
I am a creative, inventive person."
I think of an area of my life that feels limited.
As I hold this area in my awareness,
I imagine linking my mind
with the creative mind of my Higher Self.
I imagine there are no limits to
what I can have in this area.
I let myself picture many possibilities.
I expand beyond what I think I can have

and open to even greater possibilities.
I know as I think and imagine,
I create the potential
for doorways to open
and new choices to appear.
I think of something I want.
I imagine having even more,
something that will bring me joy
and expansion.
I now allow this into my life,
or something even better.
I know I deserve to have it
and I open my heart to receive it.
I take any thoughts that
tell me I can't have this.
I bring them to the light
by recognizing and identifying them.
I then change these thoughts
into positive ones,
I change them into thoughts
that tell me why I CAN create this.
I say to myself,

"I am an unlimited being. I can create whatever I want.
My choices and possibilities are expanding every day.
My dreams come true."

CHAPTER TWENTY
~*Now Let's Learn to Expand*~

The act of writing down your wishes, dreams, and goals allows your limiting beliefs, which were once concealed in your subconscious mind by your conscious mind, to become apparent. Take out your notebook where you have written all of your dreams and read it over. Notice if you diminished yourself in any of your requests. Do you find yourself asking for only as much as you believe that you need? The answers you wrote will reveal to you where most of your limiting beliefs lie. This was your opportunity to ask for absolutely anything. Did you settle? Instead of asking for a castle in Scotland or a house on the coast in California, did you request a three bedroom home in the suburbs?

If you notice that you settled for just enough, ask yourself why. Look for the beliefs hidden in your answer. When you read over your ideal relationships, did you describe the relationships that you already have because you don't want to act as though you are not happy or grateful, or did you describe a relationship with more passion, a deeper connection, communication, and support?

Did you describe the relationships you will have with friends? Did your relationships change because your day-to-day activities are different in your ideal life? Did you see yourself with financial freedom? Were you still working, or did you find other ways to spend your time that more served your passion and purpose?

Imagine what is possible in land of infinite

possibilities. Ask yourself why there is a gap between what is possible and what you asked for. Take that answer and listen to the belief hidden in it about your worth.

Sometimes we limit our wishes because we don't have a full view of what is available to us. We can't wish for something we don't know or haven't experienced. Creativity is very important. You must start to expand what you know. I recently heard an interview Oprah had with Jane Fonda. Oprah asked Ms. Fonda how she stays so sharp and quick witted. This goes against a strong belief our society holds that those things have a tendency to slow and diminish with age. She answered, "my motto in life is as follows; it is much more important to be interested than to be interesting." Jane Fonda understands the importance of imagination and the importance of maintaining a devastating thirst that can only be quenched by knowledge. Expansion is necessary if you intend to move out of what you know into something new. Expansion is something you should be doing all of the time. The world around you is continuing to expand, whether or not you are expanding with it. So if you choose to stay where you are—or even go backward—you will feel a stronger disconnect with the world around you. The longer you stay where you are, the larger the disconnect, and the more discomfort you will experience.

We tend to be comfortable with expansion only when it moves at a very small pace. We experience expansion at our yearly evaluation with our dollar-an-hour raise. We may buy a larger house as our family expands. Think about your first apartment compared to where you are living now. If you had stepped directly from that first apartment into the home you currently live in, it might have been such a large leap you may have felt uncomfortable about the transition. Instead, you worked your way from a studio apartment to a one bedroom to a two bedroom with roommates, etc. This feels much more natural and believable. The idea is to find a way to feel comfortable in a much larger leap and have belief and faith that it is possible. This next worksheet will help you prepare for larger leaps.

Chapter Twenty Worksheet
~Expansion~

*Take out a piece of paper and write "$1,000,000,"
"$5,000,000" and "$10,000,000" on it.*

*Now, begin with the $1,000,000. And, as though you
really had it, spend it on whatever you would like. Keep in mind
that you might want to look through magazines or watch tv or
movies to get ideas. Be creative! The only trick is that you must
spend it all, and it all must be spent on you. This could be
buying a new home, car, boat, art, jewelry, business etc. Next, do
the same for the $5,000,000. Start from scratch. Don't carry
over your purchases from $1.000,000. For example, the
$5,000,000 house might be bigger or in another state. Last, do
the same with the $10,000,000.*

If this was easy, try it with larger sums of money.

This exercise is designed to show you how expansion
works. If you want to manifest larger sums of money into
your life, you must first start wearing larger sums of money.
You may have found it difficult to spend the $1,000,000,
but when you finished spending $10,000,000 and revisited
spending $1,000,000, that number all of a sudden seemed
very insignificant and small. This is the idea. When you
were young and received minimum wage, you were excited!
You would think of all the ways you would spend this
incredible amount of money. As you grew, your
expectations grew. You would laugh at minimum wage.
Your expectations grew to match what you were getting all
along. Think bigger! I am here to teach you to expect more.
Don't expect "just enough." Start to expect financial

freedom. Expect to see a certain amount of money in your savings account. Expect to have a private jet or helicopter pad on the top of your mansion.

Now that you have expanded a little, it's time to rewrite your Dream sheet Chapter 18 Worksheet Page 131. Sit down and describe your ideal life, with no limitations and an expanded view. Then, once again, look to see if there are any more limiting beliefs being revealed. Then imagine for a moment that all of those beliefs are wrong.

~ Try playing the "What if" game. ~

Every time you find yourself wondering "what if something awful happens," replace it with "what if something amazing happens? What if life could be perfection unfolding?" It's easy and fun, and always allows you to feel better. "What if my husband and I fight tonight?" turns into "what if my husband and I have a wonderful time connecting and communicate with ease tonight?" "What if I lose my job and can't pay my bills?" turns into "What if I get an even better job and have enough money to go on a vacation?" What if everything works out perfectly? What if I find the relationship of my dreams and everything works out better than I could have ever imagined?

You can never know the *how*, so just leave it alone and let it be. The how only brings all of the evidence of your lack of faith. Faith doesn't need to know the how. Hold onto the thought that everything can turn around in a day, a moment, even a second. Start to expect that windfall. Get excited to see how it all turns around and, when it does, marvel in the unexpected turn of events, always in the direction you knew it would go.

First you must choose the direction. Are you worrying about all of the "what ifs." or are you getting excited about them?

When you were writing your dreams, did you notice any blocks, those *"buts"* ,*"what if's"* or *"if only's"*? What if I try and don't succeed? If only I had been born rich or didn't have a significant other and kids I would live there. But I have a mortgage, cars and people to feed; how can I release my responsibilities?

Write each dream in the same fashion shown below. As you say this dream write down any of the thoughts that arise within you that tell you why it won't be. You can use the example below to assist you.

Finding and Removing Blocks

<u>Dream</u>: *(write your dream)*
But...(I would have this dream but..)
What if.....(What if this happened and it all fell apart)
If only....(If only I had this I could have my dream)

Review what you have written. Ask yourself, could I achieve this dream if my assumptions were all wrong? What story about myself do these assumptions perpetuate? What steps would I take if I wanted to prove these assumptions wrong? Write down at least three of these steps. Repeat for each dream you wish to create.

Section Four
~*The Law of Manifesting A Holy Trinity*~
Create the vision,
cultivate the feeling,
and tell the world.

Create the life you want to have!

Over the Rainbow

CHAPTER TWENTY-ONE
~You Must believe You Deserve it!

Once you know what you want, you have to see it becoming with the same clarity that you see the sky *is* blue. Your vision and wish is filled with an overwhelming sense of conviction! It has to be because you can see nothing else; as if it is something you already have created in your experience. Nobody can tell you different. It will feel as though anyone who can't see your vision is looking at the sky and calling it green. You have to be confident enough to share with everyone that this is something that will be with a faith that says: "It already is. I just haven't revealed it yet." Let the world think you have all of the answers hidden up your sleeve.

This is where your faith will be tested. This is the only place where you have to earn anything, but not in terms of blood sweat and tears. Rather, in terms of holding onto faith through the turbulence of its unveiling.

You will have to check in with yourself from time to time. Ask yourself: do you really believe it as though it already is, or, when people start diminishing your dream, do you allow yourself to diminish with them? It is important to confidently share and express your dream with the world because you will rely on the world for assistance in making your dream a reality. If your confidence is at all faltering, the world senses it and enthusiasm diminishes.

Remember, the world is still operating under the assumption that you can't have what you want. People around you may still be holding onto those old beliefs that keep them in their safe place, the place where they know what to expect. Grow stronger every time someone tells you, you can't. Know that this is your opportunity to show them through your actions what *they* are also capable of.

The true test of faith will allow nothing to pull you away from turning your vision into a reality. You already believe you have it, so it has to be! As you follow your dream and start to see it unfolding, you will find yourself riding that wave of enthusiasm. People will want to get on that ride with you. Suddenly people will be drawn to you in ways of service and support. You just have to see it and believe it.

A great example of this comes from one of the most iconic pop stars of all time, Madonna. I was one of the millions of teenagers that grew up idolizing her. She had that passion. I couldn't wait to see what she was going to do next. Through all of the hundreds of performances, interviews I watched, one always stood out for me. I remember very vividly watching her being interviewed on one of those late night talk shows. The question that changed my life was, "What do you see yourself doing next?" Madonna's answer, "My dream has always been the same since I was a small child. I want to rule the world."

Wow! Talk about dreaming without limits. She wasn't just *thinking* of what she wanted; she was, with confidence, *telling the world* this is what she wanted. She wasn't just saying it, she believed it. Because she believed it with true faith, I believed her too! Believing it was possible for her opened my eyes to it being possible for me. This is what turns a belief into a reality. I would say that Madonna is living her dream.

"Power is being told that you are not loved and not being destroyed by it" Madonna

If you have faith and you see the end result and you know that is what you want, there are no obstacles that can stop you. There will only be opportunities to reaffirm your passion and make you stronger so you will be ready for your dreams when they are realized.

- *You must be able to overcome all obstacles and grow stronger with each hurdle.*
- *You must believe with unwavering confidence that it will be.*
- *Start to enjoy the challenge, instead of withering under pressure and allowing it to defeat you.*

The people that are closest to you, the ones that care about you the most, will be the first to tell you your dreams are not feasible, and you should be more realistic. View this opposition as your first hurdle and the sign that you are one step closer to realizing your dreams. Even your mother, the one who always said you could do anything, will tell you to stop dreaming and join the real world. This is not because she doesn't believe in you; it is because she doesn't believe in herself. If your mother has been an entrepreneur or venture capitalist, if she was Madonna, she would say *do it!* You will have to find the strength to stand on your own two feet and fight for what you believe. It is likely at points on your journey to realizing your dreams you may find yourself all alone, with nothing or nobody except your faith and your vision. Don't lose heart. Let the experience be a joyful one, and begin looking at all the ways the world is supporting you.

~Believe that you deserve to have everything that you want~

The quickest way to destroy a dream on its way to fruition is to question whether or not you deserve it. You may wonder if you are talented enough or if someone else has worked harder and is more deserving. This is never the case! You have a very special gift that is all your own and the world is waiting for you to acknowledge this gift and share it. When on purpose, you are always deserving of whatever it is that you ask for to help fulfill your mission. All of the happiness in the world should and will be bestowed upon you every second of the day as long as you are listening to and following your inner guidance!

Believing that you deserve happiness and love is a very important step. You have been programmed to push your wants and wishes aside. You have been told since you were young to put everyone else first and do what you have to, even if you don't like it: "Don't be selfish. You are just thinking of yourself. Sometimes you must sacrifice for everyone else's happiness." This way of thinking is what has created the depression and unhappiness in our world. It goes against the very core of our being. We are all here with a very special purpose and we were created specifically to contribute this gift to the world.

Doctors are prescribing anti-depressants and people are turning to alcohol or drugs to combat what society has labeled *anxiety*. Anxiety is the sensation we get when we do not honor our true self. Anxiety is the compass god has given you to tell you that you have derailed from your purpose.

Chapter Twenty-One
Worksheet
Why I Deserve My Dreams to Come True

Take all of your dreams and write them down, one by one, in the present tense. Write them down as though you already have them. For example:

- *I have found my true love. He/she adds to my life in ways I could have never imagined. We have a strong chemistry and I feel filled with passion and love.*
- *I have abundance in all areas of my life, freeing me to do what I love every day.*

Now that you have written down your dreams as though you already have them, write below each dream why you deserve it. For example:

- *I deserve to have a fulfilling relationship where my significant other treats me with loving kindness all the time because that is the way I love him/her.*
- *I deserve abundance in all areas of my life because abundance flows through me with a loving energy. Everything that I receive I give.*

Over the Rainbow

CHAPTER TWENTY-TWO

~*Dreams Into Essence*~
Starting to Recognize the Essence of the Dream

You see your dream.
You have faith in your dream.
You feel you deserve your dream.

Discovering the essence of your dream is the magic. It isn't the dream that we are looking for but the essence. This is the *feeling* part. The essence of your dream is the igniter fluid. It is what allows your inner spark to grow brighter. It is the most important part of this process.

Once you have created the thought or the vision, now you must know the feelings that are attached to having this dream manifest. The objects are just the catalyst to achieve a certain feeling or essence in our spirit. You can start to live your essence this very moment, without changing any outside circumstances. You do not need the object to start feeling the essence! This is why it is so important to be clear about the essence. Finding your essence starts with looking at your dreams and finding what it is that your soul is yearning for from the things you desire.

When you close your eyes and visualize your ideal life without limitations and you see yourself living and being that life, what feelings are you feeling? When you become your desired weight, regain your health, find your ideal mate: what does it feel like? How does it feel different? What would you do differently? Would people treat you differently? How would that feel? The magic pixie dust for making your dreams reality is just this: feel those feelings! Don't wait for the thing itself to arrive; feel the feelings as though it has arrived.

Is your dream to have a giant mansion with a helicopter pad, or your own private jet? Then the essence of the dream may be the love of traveling or venturing to new lands. Maybe your dream home has an amazing open floor plan with a large kitchen. The essence may be that you want to have perfect place for entertaining your friends and family, bringing you closer to the people you love. You may want a house on a large piece of property; the essence may be that you enjoy privacy or you like to feel more connected to nature. Look to your dreams for their essence.

~The Importance of Being Clear About Your Essence. ~

A friend once called me in the midst of a transition period in her life. Many things were changing for her all at once: her job, her residence, and her relationship were all shifting. The home was the most important thing on the agenda, as she had recently been notified that she was going to have to find a new place in a less than ideal, amount of time. She called me filled with worry. I told her that this was a beautiful blessing from above. This home was no longer serving her properly and it was time for her to transition. I asked her to tell me in detail about her ideal home.

She had already spent some time thinking about this and was able to articulate her dream home very easily. She said that she wanted an A-frame house, with the loft at the top as her special place. She knew that this loft would have a window, and the view out the window would be serenity. She wanted to see endless property, with trees and nature all around. Not surprisingly, the universe pulled out its magic wand, and because of the perfect clarity of the vision, it was able to allow this house to materialize with ease.

However, what my friend had neglected to mention was the essence of this house. She didn't mention it, because she didn't know it. This is how life works. You have to experience the lack of something in order to wish for its presence. She had called me fairly quickly after our conversation and informed me, that she had found her house. It was perfect. The husband in a two-income household had been laid off, and to help minimize expenses the couple decided to rent out the loft in their A-frame home. They would still live in the bottom, which made it even more affordable for my friend. This home had a long private driveway, and although it was on a large piece of property and had a very country feel, it was also very close to everything.

Once my friend had moved into the home she thought was the answer to all of her prayers, she realized that she needed to add to her list of home requirements. This home was missing the essence of what she wanted. It had everything as far as appeal and looks, but the family that was living downstairs also had a child. They were very loud. The essence of privacy and peacefulness she was looking to receive in the country setting was far from what she got. She felt confined to her room. Even though she could still admire the view through her window, just as she had pictured it, she couldn't enjoy it. Had she realized that privacy, peace and quiet, were what she really wanted, she could have begun living the essence of her dream immediately, even before she found her home.

When you start to live in the essence of what you want, you not only bring your dreams into reality more rapidly, you also get clarity on whether or not what you think you want is what you are actually looking for. Getting to know *you*, allows you to move in record speed toward that dream or goal you were destined for.

The essence tells you what makes you different from everyone else and you begin to discover where your passions are. Essence is the beacon that attracts all that you are wanting. Once you can recognize the essence of what you want, it is important to find ways to implement this essence into your life right now!

Chapter Twenty-Two
Worksheet

Find your list of dreams. Look at each of them. Then, ask yourself "what is the essence you will receive from your new job, meeting your soul mate, or whatever else it is you are wanting in your life right now?" Once you have the answer, write it down.

Here are a few examples:

More money = sense of financial freedom
Sports car = feeling of speed, excitement
Station wagon = wanting reliability, convenience, spacious, family
New or bigger house = feelings of more space, less clutter, privacy

Here are some essence words. Try and apply these words to your dreams.

Peace ~ security ~ freedom ~ love ~ joy ~ happiness ~ peace of mind ~ aliveness ~ inspiration ~ creativity ~ closeness ~ family ~ abundance ~ truth ~ kindness ~ compassion ~ adventurous ~ lively ~ purity ~ faith ~ traditional ~ values ~

Now look at your list and write down some ways that you can find this essence now.
For example:

- *if you are looking for a new car because you want the essence of reliability, start with getting an oil change or a tune up on the car you already have.*

- *If you are looking for speed or excitement, consider adding that in to your life in smaller ways. Indoor go-karts can go really fast. You could rent a motorcycle or a sports car for a weekend. Try snowmobiling or drag racing.*

- *If you want to live by the water but can't seem to afford it, start by taking regular trips to a local lake, river, or ocean, walking around it or sitting alongside and reading a book.*

List ten ways you can bring the essence into your life right now...

CHAPTER TWENTY-THREE

~Tell Your Dreams To The World~

You know what you want
You have cultivated the feeling and captured the essence
Now you must tell the world

The final step in the holy trinity of manifestation is announcing to the world that you intend to have (place you dream here.) Tell everyone that will listen. Say it with confidence and don't worry about explaining the how. Know with confidence that it is the work of the universe to figure out the *how*; it is your work to, dream up the impossible, capture the essence, and tell everyone that you intend to have it. The more we talk about our dreams the more we can expand and sharpen the dream.

People always have something to offer. People generally fall into one of the following categories; they are, a connector, an expert, or a server. When you tell your dream to a connector, they will right away want to connect you with someone they know that is an expert in creating those things. An expert will have unlimited information sources to help guide you and the steps that you may need to take. The server wants to help in any way they can. They are happiest when they are helping and serving others. Share your dream often from a standpoint of "It cannot fail." And notice people lining up to be a part of its fulfillment.
Expanding and changing your life in one area most likely involves expanding and changing your life in other areas. This means your circle of friends may change. The people that you have been drawn to in the past were supporting the frequency of the old you. The new you, you will want to step into a new frequency and find new people on this frequency.

The people who surround us, are here as a reflection of some part of us. It is very likely that they will all share similar beliefs about money, work, faith, life, etc. As you start to change those beliefs, you'll notice that you no longer have things in common with those people you used to share so much with. You must be okay with that. Don't try to be something that you no longer are. Be open to forging new relationships that better fit your new beliefs. As you move towards your dreams, be okay with releasing old relationships that may no longer serve you. Those old relationships tend to be like anchors holding you in place.
This does not mean that you have to dismiss people out of your life and sever the relationship completely. It just means that you will need to be aware of those friends that are not willing to grow with you and notice if you feel as though your energy and enthusiasm is decreased after spending time with them. Think about those friends that you had in high school or college. If they had stayed exactly the same, would you have anything in common with them now? If they were still living with their parents or in a sorority house with very little responsibility or thoughts of the future would they be able to feed the spirit of the person you are now? We either grow together, creating paths to our futures, or we grow apart. Either way it is okay, because letting go of old friendships that don't serve who you are leaves room in your life for new relationships that can help you grow.

Sometimes old friends may seek you out for advice as they see your life changing for the better and they want to hear some of your secrets. Be available to them. It is important to shine the light for those trying to grow with you. However, be aware of how much energy you are placing with them. When you are guiding others your energy should increase as a result. If you notice your energy being depleted, you must honor your energy first. Forming new relationships is crucial to your expansion. Without expansion, the path to your dreams cannot be revealed to you. This is the art of true surrender (releasing the old in full faith the new is on its way).

Over the Rainbow

CHAPTER TWENTY-FOUR

~*Surrender to the Universe*~
~*Practice non-attachment*~

Imagine that the path to happiness is adorned with beautiful golden pavers. As you are walking on this path, limitless wealth, fame, abundance, prosperity, wisdom, and joy are revealed to you. Once on this path, your journey becomes effortless, each step shows up clearer than the one before. Beauty is everywhere and you will have learned to speak to nature and soar with the birds. The wind blowing through the trees, the sun warming your skin, and the stars in the night sky all become an extension of you. On this path you recognize your oneness with everything, and you see your life as a piece of art that you are molding and creating.

You might be emphatically asking, "Where is this path? I am ready! Reveal it to me now!" I can assure you it is always there waiting for you. There is a key that will unlock your ability to see the path. You have always held the key in your possession and you have seen the door; you just haven't unlocked it yet.

The key to reveal all of life's wisdom, grace, and perfection is in the form of SURRENDER, to release all resistance. Surrender is accepting "what is" without the need to change it or have it different in any way.

Being free from resistance goes against the very nature of our being. Sometimes the only thing that gives us a reason to wake up every day is the excitement of the conflict that we have created. We keep the mind occupied, running its incessant chatter on thoughts of resistance. If left unmonitored, the mind will think about all the ways that the world has wronged you or is making life so difficult. When you are a passenger on the mind's journey, this is the path to suffering, stagnancy, and resistance. You feel trapped, like you keep moving in circles. You think to yourself, "This tree looks familiar, have I been here before?"

The mind runs on automatic resistance. If it is not watched over carefully, it will begin to think thoughts like "this would be perfect IF ONLY I had more money, a nicer job, a nicer car, or a happy relationship." These thoughts behave like weeds, clouding your vision and distorting your perception. With these thoughts, your path becomes overgrown and difficult to see. When you lose track of your vision it is easy to make a wrong turn and end up right where you started. You must take control of your journey. Surrender is taking a deep breath in, knowing that everything is exactly as it should be, and what is happening, is for the purpose of delivering to you your highest and best good. This can be difficult when life is testing your ability to surrender. And it will. You will make your request to the universe, announcing, "I'm ready for my good," the universe often answer's "Okay. Let's see about that."

It starts easy. You may spill your coffee and not have a change of clothes. You accept it, shrug it off, laughing to yourself while not allowing it spiral you downward ruining the rest of your day. The universe congratulates your victory by making your challenge a little more difficult.

Now your car breaks down or you lose your job. This is where you have to stay cool, calm, and collected, because if you accept it and know nothing leaves your life without something better on its way, the universe delivers that something better. You will find yourself on to the next challenge. Recognize the rewards you received from the last challenge absorbing it as a victory, not a loss.   As   you are being tested, you may have to lose all of your material possessions to prove that you truly understand that we don't really "have" anything. Labeling things as "ours" is an illusion. Things are transient and will flow in and out of your life. It is the desire to make things yours that creates resistance and suffering. The flow of life is meant to be graceful. Things come and go as energy flows freely through your experience. Resistance is the only thing that can cause backup or blocks in this flow. If you resist letting go of the old, the new can't come. You must SURRENDER.

Sometimes we can master this lesson, but still not master surrender. The final test of surrender will happen not to you but to someone or something outside of you. We sometimes have built armor and strength through our challenges, and feel as though we can take on the world, but as we witness others hurting we cannot stand by and allow it. They have a path and a lesson too and our interfering is not always assisting. The universe has a divine plan for all of us.

The final test will ask you to recognize the suffering of others as a part of their life, unfolding perfectly exactly as it should, to ask you to recognize that they are on their own journey to the promised land and that these are their lessons. The best way to support them is to give them hope to teach them to freely release and surrender.

Invite challenge; invite turmoil, invite struggle. Just call it something else. Relabeling these things with the terms change, creating space, overcoming, growth, ascension or transcendence, these experiences mean you are growing, and as you grow you are moving closer and closer to the door of unlimited abundance.

CHAPTER TWENTY-FIVE

~*Understanding Faith*~

Faith (n): confident belief in truth, value, or trustworthiness of a person, idea or thing.

To have the kind of faith that all creation emerges from, is a faith that operates one hundred percent detached from the outcome. This is a crucial component in the process of realizing your dreams. When things seem to go in a direction you didn't expect, try to view the situation as something went unexpectedly right, but in ways that are not quite apparent yet. This is how you operate under the principle of unwavering faith. This principle tells you that everything is working out in your favor, all of the time. If for just a moment you can believe that statement is true and you can imagine that there is no failure, would that change what you do? With no option of failure, what open doors would you reveal?

I have a system that I use to keep myself operating in faith. The system is simple. I wake up every morning and before I fully open my eyes I clasp my hands together and recite the following: "Thank you, God, for everything that you have ever given me."

As I say these words, I feel that gratitude in my heart for all that I have. I think about how blessed I am to have my warm bed, a cozy home, security and my loved ones healthy and happy. I think how grateful I am for the sun to warm my skin, awaken the world and breathe life into everything. If it is raining, I am grateful that the rain is washing the air and infusing life and color into all living things. I experience the sensation of gratitude for just waking up and taking that first conscious breath.

Next, I bring the essence of my dreams into my body by visualizing and feeling them as though I already have them. I state: "I surrender to the universe and know that everything that happens today is happening for my highest and greatest good. Thank you for making my dreams my reality." Finally I set my intention for the day.

Surrender is a way of life. You begin to accept your current circumstances instead of fighting them or wishing they were somehow different. When you surrender, everything begins to reveal itself as part of your path. You begin to decipher how this experience you are having fits into the big picture.

Sometimes in life we look at one experience and magnify it. We get caught up in the moment and forget our true nature. We forget who we are and move away from love to feed on fear. When this happens, the problem magnifies and grows so big that we can't see anything beyond the negative emotions and fear around the experience, like a black hole we sink into. The black hole is where we forget to be grateful and find ourselves standing in a waterfall of *poor me*. These feelings are a powerful magnet for more bad experiences; gratitude is the only way to diminish their powers.

When you fight your reality you become clouded, standing in the center of a labyrinth, all you can see are dead ends everywhere. It is as though you just stepped off the path and took a horrible detour into a dark, unloving forest full of what you don't want. It is a decision to be angry that the car got a flat tire and now you are late for work. Does anger get you any closer to solving the problem? Anger is just fighting what is. It is saying to yourself that what is happening is in some way wrong, or that you wish it wasn't happening. You must believe that everything is unfolding for your highest good. It is then that you will realize that accepting what is happening and knowing it is part of the intelligence of the universe is like finding the eye of the storm. With the whole world swirling around you in chaos, you have found your peaceful center in "What is."

From the eye of the storm, you would have seen that the car getting a flat tire and known it is all unfolding perfectly. Imagine that you had recently been thinking of an old friend, wishing you could connect with them again. This friend happened to be driving by at that moment, recognized your car, and pulled over. In the world of acceptance you would be marveling at the miracle that brought you two together. What if, you had been dreaming about the man or woman of your dreams and they found themselves in need of a car part while you were looking for fix a flat. View all circumstances as serendipity, a "happy accident." Most people struggle with finding the miracle because they are too busy finding frustration in the flat tire. Everything that happens lays the foundation to move you in perfection towards realizing your dreams. Surrender, accept, and trust. Then, you can easily see the way out of the maze toward what you wished for. Clarity is born in surrender and acceptance.

Over the Rainbow

CHAPTER TWENTY-SIX

~Attachment,
the Root of All Suffering~

Non-attachment is a necessary ingredient to manifestation. It is a virtue found in almost every faith. Yogi's practice *aparigraha*(non-attachment). This principle is one of Patanjali's eight limbs of yoga, listed in the *Yoga Sutras*, which is one of the seminal texts of Classical Yoga. *Aparigraha* is one of the *yamas*, or moral observances by which true yogi's live. To a yogi, this concept represents that we are more than what we have or the circumstances we find ourselves in. Buddha practiced non-attachment by first releasing and giving up all of his belongings, stating this as a necessary first step on the path to enlightenment. So, this is a strong observance in the Buddhist belief system.

Many modern yogi's believe that it is not the actual accumulation of wealth and possessions that hinders your ability to become enlightened; it is attachment to these things that is the culprit. If you lost everything you own today, would you feel like less of a person? Would you feel as though you lost parts of yourself? Would you mourn your losses? If you answered "yes" to any of those questions then you have not understood the mastery of non-attachment. Attachment to things creates imaginary suffering. If you believe that part of who you are is your material possessions, and you judge and decide who others are based on their possessions, then you are bound for a lifetime riddled with suffering. Everything is transient and no matter how hard you hold on, things will likely come and go. If you cannot freely release, you will experience pain as a result of the natural ebb and flow of life, coming and going.

Another way of looking at non-attachment is as complete detachment from an outcome. Not being reactive to what is happening or attached to a set of circumstances playing out in a particular way, is liberation from suffering. It is the understanding and faith that the universe knows what is best for you while recognizing that the present moment always holds everything that you need to be whole and perfect. Seeing this moment as perfection and a necessary step on the path to your highest good is embracing non-attachment.

The practice of yoga seeks to liberate us from suffering by yoking the mind, the body, and the spirit. The breath (*pranayama*, the fourth limb of the eight limbs of yoga), combined with the postures (*asana*, the third limb) forces you to be present to the experience you are having in your body in the space of a single inhalation. In the practice of pranayama, the exhale is the body's preparation for rebirth while the inhale is the rebirth itself.

Every breath brings with it a brand new life and a brand new experience. Awareness of the breath brings you fully present. It is very difficult and almost impossible to hold a challenging yoga asana and have your mind thinking about what you are going to wear later. Presence doesn't know the future exists and only sees the past as holding the story we are currently choosing to tell. It is in that story that the present or gift that is you, will be unwrapped and revealed.

In moments of stillness, the mind wants to busy itself. It will look for problems to worry about. Our minds run a stream of a constant incessant chatter that we have programmed over the years. This is not our true self. Our true self is incapable of fear, hate, anger or jealousy all perpetuated from thoughts of the imagined future. Our true self is centered in thoughts of love, bliss and joy. The mind full of thoughts is not what we wish to avoid, just taking back control over your thoughts. Let the thoughts you have be ones that serve your highest good and the good of others. Tell your past and current story as you want today to be experienced. Don't tell stories of sorrow and lack if you want today to be filled with joy and abundance.

When finding yourself running through all of the possible future outcomes of our current situation and you are filled with "what if's" and "if only's". Only say the ones that inspire you to move forward. Tell the stories where everything works out.

Life forces us to be in constant motion. We are always moving. Even stagnancy is a form of movement. Learning and growing is deemed as forward movement. Forward and ascension in this context can be interchangeable. Allow the image of an airplane moving from one air stream to another to symbolize forward movement. Turbulence is often experienced as a result of changing air streams. This is true in life as well. If you are experiencing turbulence, upsets in relationships, transitions with your job, or being forced to move from your home, view it as life shaking off all of the things that will not serve you as you move to a higher awareness. Don't fight it. Quietly sit down in your chair, buckle up, and breathe. Know you are one step closer to your destination. As you settle into the higher airstream you will once again experience smooth sailing.

"Misery is nothing but the shadow of attachment. And hence all stagnancy. The stagnant person becomes a pool——sooner or later he will sink, he flows no more."Osho

Another analogy of spiritual growth or awareness of

your true self is that of the Lotus flower. The Lotus flower is revered in many religions and belief systems as revealing the path of life, from birth through transformation and finally enlightenment. It is the symbol of health, purity, peace, beauty, and enlightenment. It is not just a glorious flower with an intoxicating fragrance, but also a reminder that beauty can sprout from the most unexpected places. The Lotus flower is born in the mud beneath a body of water.

Although it can't see the light, it manages to intrinsically find its way through the murky waters. Moving blindly through the darkness, strictly on faith, the weights begin to lift and its path becomes clear as it approaches the light. Does the lotus know that it is destined to blossom into a symbol of perfection, or is it driven by hope and faith? When the lotus finally makes its way through the waters and is bathed in the light of the sun, it blossoms into something of indescribable beauty, seemingly unscathed by the murky depths.

Our journey as a human being is similar to that of the lotus. We move through attachments and, before we experience freedom, we feel heavy and weighted down at the bottom of the water. As we start to ascend, we release these attachments, becoming more connected to our source. Unloading our accumulated baggage and becoming lighter, we eventually reach the surface and experience the warmth and glistening, radiant light of the sun.

You are well on your way. You have moved through all darkness, ready to now bathe in the light of pure happiness and joy. As you emerge into your highest self, the light illuminates you and you will blossom into a beautiful lotus flower for all of the world to see and experience. It is your time to shine!

CHAPTER TWENTY-SEVEN

~*Flowing With the River of Acceptance*~

You are either flowing with the river without judgment, enjoying the ride in trust and in faith, or you are swimming upstream and rejecting your circumstances.

It is always easy to tell which one you are doing at any given time just by experiencing your feelings. Are you feeling good or are you feeling bad? If you are rejecting your circumstances, this will never feel good. Stagnancy doesn't feel good either. The natural flow is constant movement in the direction of your dreams. If you try to stay still, you will feel as though you have grabbed onto a rock on the side of the river and are being beaten by the water as it rushes by. You always have a choice to just let go and flow with the river.

I shared an experience with a significant other I had lived with. He had a new addition to his life in the form of a boxer puppy, a vibrant, happy, lovable ball of energy. Part of our loving her was accepting that we had a new alarm clock. I knew it was time to get up when I heard her whimpering on the other side of the bedroom door opposite ours. This was her way of saying *I need to go out now*! This morning she was sounding a little more rambunctious than usual, I could hear her jumping on and off of the bed running around the room as she whimpered. I figured this meant that I should hurry. As I approached the room I began to smell something atrocious, and when I opened the door I had to cover my nose to stop myself from gagging. Diarrhea was everywhere. The walls, bed, and floor were covered. I took her outside to clean her up and told my boyfriend that there was something he should see. As he crossed the hall he immediately became enraged. This anger should have been a signal to him that he was not flowing with the river. Feelings like anger, uneasiness, guilt, and frustration do not exist in the river, so if you are experiencing those you can be sure you are either swimming upstream or holding onto the side getting battered by the current.

My boyfriend was experiencing all of those emotions at once. Instead of feeling like there was a reason for this situation and light at the other side, he was feeling a compounding sense of *why me*, which makes everything move slower.

Frustration makes things harder. Everything went wrong: he couldn't get it cleaned up; the pink towel he was using reacted with the cleaning solution and starting leaving pink marks everywhere he was cleaning. In his frustration he kept magnetizing to himself more and more to be frustrated about.

Going with the flow of the river doesn't mean that you have to be happy about cleaning up diarrhea. It is a knowing that you always have a choice to accept or reject your circumstances. In acceptance, you are always searching to see how this fits into your higher good. In this example, the bigger picture might be the warning that the dog has been getting into things that her body is rejecting. We were blessed with the early knowledge to search our environment to see what she is getting into before something more serious happened.

We have to be able to meet people where they are on the path to enlightenment.

Nothing I said to my boyfriend could pull him back into the river with me. If I am flowing with the river and you are holding onto the side, the relationship is doomed for failure. The person who is holding onto their anger and frustration is feeling as though they are not understood; they are having valid feelings that are not being validated.

As I listened to my boyfriend yelling about how much he hated the stupid dog and wished he had never gotten her in the first place, I was wishing I could leave. With each passing moment I was feeling heavier and heavier, as though weights were being placed around my ankles and I couldn't even move. I didn't want to hear him saying hurtful things about her, and I wanted to escape the rapidly decreasing energy. The dog was not out to hurt my boyfriend and had not done this on purpose. What we needed to be doing was find out why this had happened to prevent it from happening in the future. As he walked towards the front door, a fiery ball of frustrated energy, he turned back to me and said, "Why can't I just feel irritated and angry if I want to?"

I will never forget those very powerful words. I couldn't have said it better myself. He just stated out loud that it was a choice and, for whatever reason, he was choosing to feel anger and irritation instead of acceptance.
I find that this is a choice we all tend to make all too often. I granted him his wish and so did the universe. When he left, I simply wished that my home stay peaceful, and if my boyfriend needed excuses to be angry to please give him excuses away from my home. Two days later, I get a text from him, a picture of the inside of his car. He had taken his dog with him that day for work and she had had a similar episode all over the inside of his car. The universe is so kind and loving that it always delivers to you exactly

what you ask it to. Once again, he had a reason to be angry and irritated. Zeroing in on one event and allowing your feelings about that event to magnify the situation is never the answer.

CHAPTER TWENTY-EIGHT

~*Always Say "Yes"*~

The say "yes" principle is simple. You must always say "yes" to every opportunity that arises, trusting that you are safe and that every experience is a gift from the universe waiting to be revealed. A "yes" will always take you one step closer to the life of your dreams. Remember that just this morning you surrendered to your higher power, trusting that everything that happens today is for your higher good. If you have asked the universe for something and the universe is trying to deliver it, you have to be ready, willing, and able to accept it.

We have developed habits that feel comfortable. When opportunities arise that don't fit within the confines of our habits, we respond with an emphatic "no, I don't want anything different," so that is exactly what we get. If you feel like there is something missing and you want more than just going through the motions, you have to start by saying "yes."

How can an invitation to go ice fishing take you closer to the vacation of your dreams, or how does meeting a friend for ice cream lead you to the man of your dreams? Remember, it isn't up to you to decide how to get from A to B. There is never a need to connect the dots. There is only a need to have faith that the universe IS conspiring for you. Learning to make a request and then release it is an art. Once you have released it, you have to be willing to accept your request being answered, however it shows up.

You think to yourself, "I want to be able to afford a

vacation." Picture the vacation. Get very clear on the details. Is it a tropical place? Do you want to experience a new culture? Are you looking to relax by a pool or be active and tour museums? Once you know what you want and you can imagine what it feels like to already have it, you must release it and wait to see how it shows up. Then be prepared to receive it. Know it is on its way and get excited to find out how it is going to get there. But try not to have an expectation of how it will arrive! If you start to plan and have an expectation that it can only show up for you a certain way, you will only find more and more disappointment.

At first, it may seem as though things aren't working out. This isn't at all true. In fact, it is very much the contrary. Things are working perfectly, just not the way you expected them to. Maybe to get this vacation, you have decided you had to work extra hard save the extra money. You also decided to cut out all extra activities that may cost you money. So you decline all invitations to do fun things with your friends and you never quite get enough money because, due to the imbalance in your life and the lack of trust and faith in the universe, you kept encountering situations that cost you money like your car breaking down, house expenses, etc.

Instead, make the request and continue to do what you do every day with balance, trust, and faith. Begin putting a little bit of money away and shop for books about the places you want to travel. Get clearer on your vision and more excited as you look online for travel packages. Accept that invitation out to dinner. At the dinner table, you tell your friends about your plans to travel and all of the places you want to see, describe it so they can see it too. Watch as the miracles unfold. Maybe, you find out that one of your friends has a time share in that same place and won't be able to use it this year, and they offer it to you free of charge.

We are all programmed at an early age that everything has strings attached to it. If it comes too easily, it must be no good. We might even get concerned when things start going to good, bracing ourselves for it to take a turn for the worse. This is just not how the universe operates! We have all been taught wrong! Life is good. Life always works out, and in the end we always get what we want once we are in a ripe and fit place to receive it. Say what you want and start to trust that it is coming. Be aware and look for the steps as they reveal themselves. Always say "*yes*."

If you can see it, you can have it,
Visualize your life into reality

I had once dreamed of a cruise. I started to visualize myself sitting by the pool basking in the sunshine, blue skies without a cloud in sight, surrounded by water. I envisioned visiting tropical places, imagining warm sand beneath my feet and drinking from a coconut right off the tree. I started looking through magazines and pulling out pictures that seemed to embrace the ambiance I was looking for. At the time I had absolutely no logical steps as to how it would arrive. I had nothing but faith. I was in a business that was barely getting by and logically should not be contemplating a vacation. I had never been on a cruise, or even a vacation for that matter. Being completely rational, I really didn't have any reason to expect I would be going on one now. However, the thought made me happy and feeling good is the path to forward movement, growth, and expansion.

Here is an example of how the unimaginable can come to be. I simply said "*yes*" and kept moving in the direction of feeling good. A couple of weeks later, a friend of mine invited me to a birthday party. She was about fifteen years older than I, a work colleague who had been going through a tough transition in her life and had come to rely on me for guidance throughout this transition. The birthday boy was twenty years older than I, and of course most of his guests were in that same age range. It would have been easy for me to say no to this invite just based on feeling awkward. I never let that stop me, though.

Towards the end of the evening, a friend of the birthday boy's family showed up. He was closer to my age and immediately drawn to me. We talked a little due to the fact that our ages gave us something in common. We exchanged numbers and talked from time to time. I had never once mentioned to him that I was wishing to someday soon take a cruise. A few weeks later, I received a text from him asking me if I wanted to go on a cruise to the Caribbean. Expecting that he was being facetious, I responded with "absolutely." As it turned out he was quite serious. He was planning a cruise and was looking for someone to go with. It wasn't going to cost him any more for the cabin to bring me along. He really just wanted a companion and he had promised no strings were attached. I ended up trusting in the universe that this was how my request was being delivered and ended up having the best vacation of my life, all expenses paid, with no strings attached.

I wonder how hard this is for some of you to read. You are thinking, absolutely there were strings attached. That guy wanted something. Who just gives without expecting something in return? We only see it this way when we are talking about receiving. When we are talking about giving, I am sure all of you could tell endless stories about how many times you have unselfishly given with no need for reciprocation or acknowledgment. I am always looking for ways to give because giving time, money, love, and energy feels good. On the other side of giving there has to be a receiver. There has to be the completion of the circle. Why not receive and allow the giver the opportunity to feel good?

Yoga is a practice that is grown and nurtured from within and rarely looked at as a group effort. When your legs are shaking and fatigued and you feel like you can't hold on for one more second you battle with will power and perseverance but rarely do you search for help. You endure and push through, just like you do in life. One day as I struggled to hold a posture, not giving up, a teacher said to me, "Place your hand on your knee to stabilize your leg." When I hesitated, the teacher added, "Go ahead, do it. One thing I have learned in life is never turn down help or money." So beautifully spoken, as I placed my hand on my knee, I was grateful for the assistance and wondered why I didn't take the assistance being offered more often.

Over the Rainbow

CHAPTER TWENTY-NINE

~Life begins at the end of your comfort zone~
Neale Donald Walsch

We can't grow and expand into something new, if we don't step outside of what we know. Growth and expansion emerge from saying "yes" to new experiences. Imagine that every invitation is really the universe placing that next step in front of you on the path to your dreams, even if that connection seems almost impossible to make. It is important to start paying attention to which doors are opening and which doors are closing. Try always to walk through the ones that are opening, especially if you are unsure about what is on the other side, and accept that the doors that close are closing for your own good. Know that the more uncomfortable the invitation, the more outside of your comfort zone, the more likely you will grow and expand by saying yes.

I think of the comfort zone as a big circle drawn all around you, with you standing in the center. Within that circle is all that you have come to know and expect in your life. This includes your day-to-day routine of waking up and brushing your teeth, making coffee, getting ready for work, driving to work, lunch at the usual places in the usual way, driving home, and going to bed. You may expect a few extra activities such as dinner, a movie, the occasional vacation.

Included in this circle are the relationships with those

closest to you, the ones that you let in. It all fits in the realm of your expectations your comfort. Think for a minute about what you allow into your circle. How big is your comfort zone? Is your circle expanding year after year or is it growing smaller? You will know this by looking at your life a year ago and seeing it now. How many new things have you tried? How many new friends do you have? Has your job or responsibilities changed?

Right outside of your comfort zone is another circle. This circle holds an entirely different life. This is the life you wish you had, the life that you have always dreamed of. This life has very different day-to-day activities. It may be in a different city or it may be based on different expectations. It might include having more money or traveling to more exotic locales. Maybe it involves a talent that you have always dreamed of revealing to the world. This second circle holds a more expanded version of you, your true self. This new version of you brings you one step closer to experiencing true happiness and joy, one step closer to the life you were meant to have.

You were meant to be happy. You were meant to express love all of the time with every action, every thought, every ounce of your being, with absolutely no exceptions. It is very unnatural for us to live in fear, hate, unhappiness, and untruth. It goes against the very fiber of our being. As you move outside your comfort zone and into this new paradigm, you bring leave the old version of you behind as you expand into something more. This is what life should constantly consist of: shifts outside of what we know into more of ourselves.

As children, this is very normal. We were constantly expected to grow and experience new things. It may have been uncomfortable at times, but we had support, people telling us that this was what we had to do. As children, we only knew forward movement. There was no possibility of failure. When we were little we were always applauded for our efforts, so we didn't yet develop the negative, fearful thoughts or the concept of failure. Our first step, even if we fell afterwards, left people overjoyed. They didn't view it as a failure. When we fell, they recognized it as one step closer to the goal.

You had to take large leaps of faith and trust as you moved and grew. However, it was easier back then. Remember when you learned to drive, your first job, your first apartment? These were scary steps. You knew you had to do it to become a contributing member of society, but people and society also told you to beware of this and look out for that. At this stage, you heard what they said and chose to believe a different belief. You chose to hear how difficult it would be to make ends meet when you are on your own, and yet you still had faith that you could do it. This was likely not difficult, because so many people around you were doing the same thing. You were able to say, "If they can do it, I certainly can."

~The World needs you to live on purpose!~

As you get older and step outside of the comfort zone, the forward movement takes you into uncharted territory. There will not always be someone else there doing the same thing. Even if there is someone there, you can't always find that connection that tells you "if they can do it so can I." You may even hold these people with such a high regard that you believe you can't ever meet their standards. You believe they have something special that you lack.

We are all connected to the same source. All you have to do is tap in. It is when you stop tapping into source and stop expanding that you stay stagnant and forget what happiness feels like. Perhaps you find a place that is comfortable and sit back, watching other people living your dreams, and imagine they have something different from you. They deserve it and you don't. This thought is somehow reassuring, because it explains why you aren't there and they are. But it's a lie. It is a lie that you are telling yourself. The only difference between you and them is that they had an undying faith. They were able to create a dream, a vision, and believe that it would be realized. They didn't listen to the naysayers, they didn't lose faith, and they fearlessly stepped into the unknown outside their comfort zone.

When transcending through your comfort zone to a higher version of yourself, you absolutely cannot look outside of yourself for reassurance. You will only be able to see and experience your truth by going inward, getting quiet, and dismissing all fearful thoughts. You have to start to connect with your feelings. It takes incredible awareness to consistently check in and see whether you are operating from a place of love or fear at any given moment. When you are operating from love, you are connected with your true self, your divine self, your intuition. If you follow the guidance that comes from that place, you cannot fail.

The greatness detector

We have confused that the feeling that we get in our stomachs, that feeling that we have labeled intuition, as a signal that something bad is about to happen. We associate it with fear and we associate fear with bad things. However, if you think about the most powerful life-changing events anyone could ever have, such as moving out of your parents' house, driving for first time, having a baby, getting married, starting a new job, going on stage to be honored or awarded for a personal achievement, giving a speech that touches people's lives, you might realize that all these are often accompanied by that feeling. All of the greatest people we know and now honor with holidays felt this feeling before entering into their greatness. This is why I have come to call this feeling *the greatness detector*. Every time in my life I find myself in a position where I am overwhelmed, experiencing a quickening of the heart, sometimes erratic off beats, activation of the adrenals in the fight or flight mechanism, tight chest, and shaky hands, I know this is an indicator that I am on the verge of expanding into my greatness. This becomes the test for me to stay strong and know greatness is to be had at the other side.

Start to look for these opportunities and, when they arrive, instead of fearing failure step right into your greatness. The only failure we can ever have in life is if we allow ourselves to be defeated by fear before we even start. Sometimes we don't even realize just how boxed in we have become. We have boxed ourselves into a very uncomfortable existence and allowed fear to keep us from moving outside of the box. Think of the people who stay in abusive relationships. They don't stay because they are happy. They stay because it is what they know, and what they know is comfortable. The biggest problem is that it was usually it was their own belief that created their environment. So even if they escape this abusive relationship, if they don't work on discovering what the belief is and changing it, they will just find another abusive relationship. People, by nature, don't like change. The belief has to change first. Then they find the faith that life is meant to be good. Lastly, they listen to their greatness detector and step into the world of the unknown.

What if fear could be removed entirely from your life? Would it change the way you live?

Fear of the unknown is too vast and all encompassing. The entire day could be encumbered with ways to avoid what we perceive as failure, pain, or a broken heart, when all that would really be accomplished is avoiding life! Instead of living in fear of what the future holds, can you live for now and what this moment holds? The goal is to consume each moment entirely, until you can truly taste all the flavors, even the ones you didn't expect.

There are people who push this to the extreme. They have chosen to conquer all of their fears by facing them head on. These people jump out of planes or climb mountains, taking on the elements and pushing their bodies to extremes. These people do not respond to fear by contracting back to their comfortable space. They see fear and recognize it for what it is and move into the fear head-on.

On the other end of the spectrum are people who never leave their state because they are afraid to get on an airplane. Which of these two people will die first, and from what? Who had the more fulfilling life? Choose not to be ruled by fear. Be ruled by passion, love, happiness, joy, and being of service. See all that lies just outside of your circle and step outside of what you know to experience it. When you live from your truth, fear dissipates.

Ernest Holmes wrote this quote in his sermon by the sea and it continues to inspire me each time I read it. *"Find me one person who no longer has any fear of the universe, or of God, or of man, or of anything else and you would have brought to me someone in whose presence I can sit and fear shall vanish like clouds before the sunlight."*

As I read this I hear him saying that, removing fear and living in faith, would not only change my life, but it would change the life of everyone I come in contact with. Each person I met would experience the same feeling of freedom from worry just by being in my presence. The work we do to free ourselves from fear can is never selfish. It can affect the world in a positive, inspiring, uplifting way.

There are times when we slip back into being unconscious and find suffering and misery as we fall into the victim mode. Sometimes it is easy to get caught up in feelings of "the world is happening to me." We need to recalibrate from time to time, just like rebooting a computer to clear out its cookies and search history. At these times, stop and step away from it all and find your truth.

Over the Rainbow

CHAPTER THIRTY

~*Fear vs. Intuition*~

If you can live in the moment and remove fear, lying dormant beneath that fear is intuition, your true self, your guide. It has always been there waiting, wanting to reveal the road to eternal happiness but, its whispers couldn't be heard because the fear spoke so much louder. It is always easy to distinguish between the messages that are fear based and those coming from your intuition, because the fear is the one that arrives first and is always loudest voice in your head. It is likely the message running through your head all day.

Your intuition is impossible to hear through all the noise. Think of your fearful thoughts as little children; they just want to be heard and acknowledged, searching for some sort of validation before you can escape the wrath of their repetitive warnings. Once you have given them your full attention and reassured them that everything is okay, they run off and play again. Listen in the stillness and you will hear your truth.

Intuition speaks in a gentle, reassuring and loving voice. It is a peaceful, loving guide, always lighting the path to the right place at the exact moment to connect you to the source and create the future the universe has been instructed to create by its co-creator: you. There are no boundaries or times when intuition is not available. There are only times when fear is speaking louder and you forget how to quiet it down to listen for the whispers. Peaceful guidance is always accessible from one moment to the next, with no exceptions.

Fear will tell you don't do it, stop, lock your doors and stay inside. Fear can take over every cell in your body, creating illness, disease, and unhappiness as you move away from the source. Anxiety, fear, stress will surely diminish your light. The immune system can't work as efficiently in negative emotions. The cells in the body need light to recharge, re-energize, and heal themselves. Fear is the darkness where cancers are born.

When the fearful thoughts arise, recognize them for what they are and know that you have nothing to fear because you are a being of love and always guided by intuition. Let love, peace, truth and happiness be the igniter fluid that allows your light to shine and continue growing brighter. Try to send love to your fearful thoughts and remind yourself that you are always safe as long as you are in a place of love in your heart. When you are in love, your vibration is so high and your light is so bright that you are untouchable.

Dwelling on the past and wishing you could change it is the only mistake you have ever made.

Know that everything that you do every day is perfect. How many times have you asked yourself, "Was that the right decision?" Thinking and rethinking all of the different scenarios and how they could have played out if you had only done one thing differently. This does not serve in growth from this moment forward, and this is where suffering comes in. Knowing that every decision is the right decision at that time in your life will help you grow and reach towards the next level of happiness and joy. Wondering "what if?" has absolutely no benefit to it. It simply makes the past wrong. It says that you are not sure you made the right decision. It says, if only I could go back. But you can't! You can't go back and change your decision or do something differently. It already happened. Accepting this moment as perfect just as it is, means you have to also accept every single moment prior to this moment, because they all were a part of creating the now. You did the best you knew how to do in that moment. All you have now is this breath, and you CAN choose to become without limitations, absolutely anything, in this breath.

"Be the change you wish to see in the world." Mahatma Gandhi

You are the creator. The words that Gandhi spoke are powerful words that rule my life. I do not look at life to deliver circumstances to me that are pleasing. I walk into circumstances with the attitude that I will be the change, and I watch the circumstances change because of me. I am the beginning and the end and in control of my experience.
Do you become your surroundings or do your surroundings become you? Do you change who you are and what you believe depending on your circumstances and who you are surrounded by? Are you the chameleon who doesn't really have his/her own identity outside of what they feel they are supposed to act like in any given situation? If you find yourself becoming your surroundings, then you are not living your truth in that moment. By not living your truth, you are not being of service in that situation.

Let's say you knew what you wanted. You asked the universe to deliver it to you. The universe delivered it and you, said "YES," and when you got there, you forgot your truth. You forgot what your higher good wanted and you started to walk and talk like you thought the people around you wanted to hear and see. It is then that what you wanted disappears. It's still right there waiting for you to return to it, but you can't see it through all of your disguises.

You must love yourself before you are able to express your love out unto the world; an unconditional kind of love, the kind that loves all of those things you deem imperfections. It is impossible to feel loved if you don't trust that you are enough for the world exactly as you are. Your values, experience and stories create you and your contribution to the world. Every situation is an opportunity to grow and expand or to create expansion for those that surround you. Don't diminish yourself and choke down the words you want to say, fight the urge to hug someone or lend them a hand, you might be exactly what the world needed in that breath.

Ask yourself, "How do I feel right now? Do I feel good or bad?" If you feel good, you are on the right path and expressing who you truly are. If you feel bad, you are most likely not being true to you. To "Be the change you wish to see in the world," you must always hold true to who you are. This quality is mesmerizing and intoxicating. People are drawn to it. You will notice everyone else becoming the chameleon and changing ever so slightly to the much more powerful energy that is exuding from you. They will want what you have and, like putty in your hands, you can design the situation however you want to.

CHAPTER THIRTY-ONE

~*Remembering Who We Really Are*~

When the breath of life first enters our body, we are infused with the substance of the universe, sometimes referred to as *prana* or vital, life force energy. This loving, pure essence radiates from our being and is able to change the world around us as it expands.

There is a strong feeling of emotional connection that fills the room as a baby is born. It is a difficult feat to escape the pure essence and innocence. The baby brings this glow to the mom, dad and everyone else that comes in contact with her. This is what we are made of, a pure essence of love. At some point on the baby's journey, the surrounding energies start to become too strong and begin to diminish her purity and recognition of the truth. She starts to forget that she doesn't need to find love outside of herself because she already is all of the love she will ever need. This is when her life begins to be altered. She then begins to absorb the belief in her surroundings, becoming a victim of her environment.

This becomes our predetermined fate. We all suffer this fate, a fate granted to us from the events that occur while we are being introduced to life and all it encompasses. These are the events that happen before we have control over our own choices, while we are still dependant on others to provide our necessities for survival. Realizing your dreams shows you how to overcome that powerfully intrinsic pull and start right where you are, to change your path completely. As you move in the direction of your dreams you will begin to remember the love that is you.

Peaceful, serenity and blissful existence is what we are all looking for. We have that glimpse of our true selves always lingering in the back of our minds. As we move further away from our true self, we experience pain and discomfort. When we move in the direction of remembering, we feel good and joyful. However, we spend little, if any, time per day thinking about how to achieve moving in the direction of truth. It's much more likely that we are thinking about the lack of love and happiness in our life and searching for it outside of ourselves. The more we search outside of ourselves, the more we find other people's limiting beliefs stunting us and hindering our path. The truth is always available to you and is always right where you are standing. As often as you can, try to take a moment and do with that moment something that allows your soul to flourish.

With that in mind I had taken a trip to the ocean recently to think, as I know that the greatest wisdoms of all lie in the powerful vastness of a beauty that needs no explanation. I sat on the beach, more present than I had ever been, watching as sailboats disappeared into the horizon. For a moment I had no thoughts of my past or my future. I dug my feet into the sand and drew into my lungs the deepest breaths I could, allowing the air to circulate throughout my entire body. I was trying to take it all in. It was then that I wondered quietly to myself, "Am I a lost soul? Have I come here in this moment in search of guidance or an answer of some sort?" I felt so small and insignificant sitting there, watching the sky as it touched the ocean so far away, that I could hardly conceive of the distance. I had traveled quite a distance myself and was now looking for answers, but I wasn't sure of the questions.

"Okay, I am here, now what?"

I had felt guided to that spot as though there were giant arrows everywhere directing me there. I don't know what I expected: a message in a bottle or a jet to write something in the sky? Maybe I expected a sage with the answers to the meaning of life to stumble upon me. So I sat and I waited. I watched the surfers hustling to get into their wet suits before they missed the wave. I watched people jogging, bike riding, and sailing. Still feeling very alone and unnoticed, I sat in silence and wondered, can they see it anymore? Do they see what I see? Are they thinking about their plans for the evening or what had transpired earlier that day, while right in front of them sits one of the most mesmerizing visions of sheer life force? Below the ever-changing, constant movement on the surface of the ocean there is a vast ecosystem. How do we, as a whole, stop? Just stop and truly see, with no veils of illusion, through glasses of pure gratitude, that we have been given this moment, whatever it may be, so make the best of it. Don't devour the moment; instead let it linger on your tongue, allowing it to dissolve slowly so you don't miss the sound of the waves crashing upon the beach or the birds singing in the distance. There might be a special message just for you hidden in the waves, but your mind was too bogged down with the constant, meaningless chatter to hear it. I guess I had received the message I was meant to receive! I didn't need a blimp after all, floating above me with giant words along the side saying: Your entire life exists as a series of moments! All we ever have is this very moment, and right as we experience it, it is gone. This moment carries with it love, peace, happiness, truth, wholeness, and perfection, always.

This message became clear to me as soon as I was able to I remove all of the everyday routines and expectations, to sit in solitude and just be. This is why I urge you to try and find that time, the time in your day where you can connect with what really is. Some people find this through meditation, yoga, walking in a garden, being with Mother Nature. How do you connect to the present moment?

I have practiced and taught yoga for over 16 years. Yoga is, by definition, a way to liberate from self-induced suffering by learning to quiet the mind and be present. It is the yoking or joining of the mind, the body and the spirit. Every class starts with a meditation, a quieting of the mind, a simple reminder of who you really are. The yoga mat can become, for some, a sacred place. It is their church, synagogue, temple, vihara or any other place of worship. The goal while practicing yoga is to stay in that state throughout your practice. At the end of the class, you center yourself in a savasana (corpse pose, lying flat on your back with eyes closed) and connect with any revelations you have received during class. This can be a powerful transformation for people.

Yoga can be an escape from our daily bombardment of technology. As we function in society, we may find that every time the mind has a moment of peace we find ourselves looking for a distraction. This is often why we text, call, or connect to social media to see what everyone else is doing. This often leaves us feeling disconnected and uneasy. We are looking at other people's lives through the veil of illusion created by the person displaying themselves. You see only the portion they want to display, and you take this as the whole. Then you compare their displayed life to your complete life, and you may feel a sense of disappointment. This is self-induced suffering.

Your lives are busy. Sometimes we purposely keep our lives incredibly full, because if it were to quiet down even for a moment, you may have to feel how very disconnected to your true happiness you have become. You keep busy, rushing from one thing to the next, never addressing how your soul is being nourished from moment to moment.

You have attached yourselves to the material world and, in doing so, completely detached from your greater happiness that is derived from the spiritual realm. I urge you to find time to stop, reconnect, and redefine what your happiness is. You are living what you thought at one time you wanted and would make you happy. Now that you have arrived here, it might be time to readdress what your happiness really is.

Very few great human beings, pioneers of forward movement in our society, lived by society's rules. Instead, they followed their own path and paved their own way through this world. It is a wonderful thing to have rules to follow and a path to guide you. However, it is a sign of greatness to recognize your true calling and veer off the path and create new rules if necessary. It is not easy to go against the grain. You have to stay strong inside your spiraling, impenetrable vortex of pure faith. The world will tell you, you are wrong. They will ask you to stop being different and be more like them. How will you come to know your *dharma*, the Sanskrit word for one's true path? It starts by getting quiet and going within.

~Make the return to your true nature and remember who you are~
"Do ordinary things with extraordinary love."
Mother Teresa

Take Mother Teresa's advice, Do the ordinary things that fill your day with extraordinary presence. Avoid those moments of unconsciousness. Sometimes we find ourselves floating through life on autopilot. We have all been in the car and drove somewhere, only to arrive and realize we have no recollection of the drive.

I had created a list of small tasks that I wanted finished this one afternoon. I was going to run to the bank, make a few calls, and grab a cup of tea. I had the deposit for the bank next to me and had set off on my mission. The calls I had to make had been ones I was avoiding, and I had placed an incredible amount of stress over making these calls. I started to make the calls while getting tea, and was still on the phone as I drove to the bank to make the deposit. When I arrived back to my business, the deposit was nowhere to be found. Frantically, I looked everywhere. I went back into the coffee shop to retrace my steps. I was panicking.

After about fifteen minutes of this, I wondered if it could be possible that I had dropped off the deposit and just didn't remember. I went back to the bank and, sure enough, I had just been there thirty minutes earlier and dropped off the deposit.

I was completely unconscious. How often are we unconscious? How many times have you been driving somewhere and all of the sudden you realized you got on the freeway heading north when you intended to drive south? You had switched into autopilot and your subconscious took over taking you home. When we slip into an unconscious state, the habitual mind takes over. How much of life is missed on autopilot?

To be connected to source you have to remain conscious *all of the time*. You have to recognize those moments in the day that are so routine that you no longer have to be present as you move through them. To do ordinary things with extraordinary love, try brushing your teeth, and instead of planning your day, experience the toothbrush connecting with every tooth and bring loving energy into that interaction. Think that you are cleaning your teeth to reveal healthy, happy teeth. Try to be present as you flow through mundane activities like doing the dishes or laundry. It is in those moments of presence that the mind becomes quiet and you can connect with your true self and receive your divine guidance.

Notice if you move through these activities experiencing negativity. Telling yourself that nobody in your family cleans up after themselves and you feel taken advantage of, or self-talk about how much you hate doing these mundane chores will never produce anything productive. All this does is release negative and unloving energy into your space, to be absorbed by the walls and you will feel it later.

With this presence and loving state of mind, you begin to see the connection between yourselves and every living thing. Nothing can be achieved alone. Just as you play a role in creating the dreams of those around you, there are so many people involved in making your dreams come true as well. As my friend Jason Coleman, once said, "Although you and I are in different parts of the world, there is no distance between us. We all vibrate at frequencies that affect others, which in turn affects us. We are all cut from the same cloth. In actuality there is no separate *you* and separate *me*. We are truly one. I cannot say that I am truly at peace if my left hand is in peace, while my right hand is in agony. Our goal is for all beings to realize that we are all cut from the same LOVE, that huge universal love that binds everything together. There are so many "independent" pieces of love floating around, feeling separate, when they really are all one. Holding them all together is a mysterious glue, the most magical element that we call The Law of

Attraction, which allows them to manifest anything they want. Whatever I want takes not just me to achieve it, but the help of many others. Those others all have their own wants. Managing all of the requests put to The Law of Attraction is the "universal mind." Without bias, it sorts everything out and gives everyone what they have requested from the law of attraction."

The recipe for manifestation, simplified

As you think the thought, you start to experience the feeling in the body. The feeling you are trying to experience is the feeling you would have if you already had this thing in your life. So you think the thought and you feel the feeling, then you simply take the action.

At first the action might be unclear, so it is only necessary to say the words. Tell everyone that this is what you intend on having. Speak it with an unwavering confidence, as if you already have it. Eventually the more you think the thought, feel the feeling, and say the words, the actions will show up and you will know what steps to take to move you in the direction of your dream. The holy trinity has a secret ingredient. The secret ingredient is the most powerful part, the thing that transforms the way the recipe melts in your mouth. This ingredient is gratitude.

CHAPTER THIRTY-TWO

~*The Key to Happiness is in Gratitude*~

You *must* find gratitude that your dreams have been answered even before they have been. Gratitude is a state of being and a way of life. It is easy to be grateful for our loved ones, friends, kids, the warm bed where we rest our heads, and the food that nourishes us every day. The problem is to also find gratitude for those things that haven't happened yet or for those transforming situations in our life that brought us to our knees in pain and hurt. Those situations, as painful as they are, have opened your heart, tested your faith, and allowed you to feel in places you may have been numb. Find gratitude for those things that forced you to grow stronger and more determined.

It is important to see the things in your life that you don't like as an opportunity to view the contrast in order to learn more about what it is that you do like. The passing moment is the soil of gratitude. From each moment grows appreciation for what you have right now, before it is gone. Gratitude is one of the greatest healing emotions. It can bring your thoughts and feelings into a beautifully transforming symphony of truth. It can melt the toughest situations or heighten the ordinary moments to profound realization. Gratitude opens the chambers of our hearts, allowing us to really feel while we are alive.

Start practicing gratitude. When you find yourself

upset by a situation, see if you can find something in that situation to be grateful for. Wake up with gratitude and go to bed with gratitude. I do this every morning and night. Before my eyes open in the morning, I infuse my body with the sensation of gratitude for this day! At night before bed, I reflect on the day and think of all of the things I have to be grateful for on that particular day. Keep a gratitude journal, giving yourself the opportunity to reflect throughout the day or before they go to bed on what you have gratitude for.

With practice gratitude becomes easy. When you trip on a crack in the sidewalk, you are grateful for the opportunity to be more present. You may have been unconsciously walking unaware of your surroundings. Instead of being angry when your significant other shows up late for a date, try to be grateful that you have someone with whom you share your life.

Creation Starts with Vision

Have you lost the ability to daydream somewhere along the path to adulthood? Your creativity and imagination are two very important keys to unlocking the door to your true potential. It is so important to try and picture what you want, becoming more and more clear about what it looks like.

Think Twice Before You Think

It all comes down to this: what do you want, and are you an awake, aware, in love, grateful and conscious human being? Are you saying yes to new experiences and constantly expanding into more? Did you remember that you are a vibrant, energetic, important, loving and deserving part of the whole?

Your heaven *does* exist. It has been there all along right in front of you, just waiting for you to give it permission to reveal itself.

The world is waiting for who you are becoming

So hurry up!!

Made in the USA
San Bernardino, CA
17 January 2014